DOMES OF DELIGHT

The History of the Bradford
ALHAMBRA

by

Peter Holdsworth

BRADFORD LIBRARIES AND INFORMATION SERVICE

ISBN 0 907734 18 9
Published by Bradford Libraries and Information Service 1989
Produced by City of Bradford Metropolitan Council Printing Unit
Copyright © 1989 Peter Holdsworth

DOMES OF DELIGHT

British Library Cataloguing in Publication Data
Holdsworth, Peter
  Domes of Delight : the history of the Bradford Alhambra.
  1. Great Britain. Theatre, history
  I. Title II. Bradford Libraries and Information Service
  792'.0941

Contents

Illustrations

Panel Inserts

Illustration Credits

Foreword

There were three flourishing theatres in the Bradford of my youth: the raucous Palace, the elegant Prince's and the sumptuous Alhambra. I was born too late to savour the delights of the Empire and the Royal, both of which had been converted into picture-houses long before I reached a theatre-going age. Queen of them all of course was the Alhambra, by virtue of its size, its impressive architecture, its dominating situation in the centre of the city, and the undoubted quality of the varied entertainment that was presented on its stage.

For a working-class lad growing up in The Slump, coppers were hard to come by; and it was to be years before I could go to any theatre as a paying customer. But quite early on I discovered (due to what started then and has since turned out to be a lifetime's devotion to show business) that you could get a modicum of delight for absolutely nothing, if you were patient, blessed with an acute sense of hearing, and had a lofty disregard for Bradford's climate. The secret was to linger outside the great dock-doors that stood between the stage door and the entrance to the Morley Street Cinema, and opened directly on to the wings of the Alhambra's acting area. Here, with one ear pressed against the green-painted wooden boards and the other sealed off by a fingertip, you could hear the orchestra playing in the pit, a reasonable amount of singing and patter, and (one of the most satisfying sounds in the world to my young ears) the roars of applause from the delighted audience inside. You could also meet the artistes in person as they left the theatre, if your meagre resources could stretch to the purchase of a cheap autograph album. I have mine to this day. In it is the last autograph that the renowned American duettists Layton and Johnstone ever gave, for their week in Bradford during the mid-thirties saw the dissolution of that famous partnership. On the Saturday night, via my favourite scene-doors, I heard them sing at the piano in perfect harmony the last song they ever performed together: it was the Rogers-Astaire number *The Continental.* I waited out in the street afterwards in pouring rain, and they graciously gave me their signatures on one and the same page of my book before they went their separate ways. As far as I know, they were never to meet again.

Later on (earning my living by this time) I was paying my way, and could frequently be found perched high up in 'the gods'. From this elevated position I saw great plays, heard great music and watched, enthralled, many of the foremost luminaries of the variety and music-hall stage. Once you start thinking about those star-studded programmes the memories crowd back thick and fast. Thus I recall — instantly and with intense pleasure — Tommy Handley in *The Disorderly Room,* Ted Ray *Fiddling and Fooling),* Norman Evans *(Over the Garden Wall),* the great Frank Randle *('By gow, I've supped some ale toneet!')* and the incomparable Gracie Fields, who did half a dozen cartwheels round the forestage during her rendering of *Put Your Shoes On, Lucy!* Then there were the big bands: Jack Hylton, Henry Hall, Harry Roy, Roy Fox, Billy Cotton and all the others ... but I could go on for ever, for the place always held me spellbound.

A grizzled Bradfordian, whose wit and wisdom were superior to his gift of tongues, once told me that the theatre's name was Arabic for 'the home'. This was an erroneous translation, as you will learn within these pages. His version may have been inaccurate but it has lived in my mind through the mists of time, so I shall forever think of the Alhambra as a genuine *home:* a dwelling-place for leading players in memorable plays, glorious voices in grand opera, extravagant pantomime, the delicacy of ballet, luscious musicals, and — perhaps above all, in the dark days of war — a temporary abode of all the famous names in the world of variety. It has always been for me, and will remain, a palace of magic.

We are fortunate indeed in having Peter Holdsworth as our guide and mentor on this fascinating theatrical journey. He is an esteemed critic, a highly valued local historian and a man for whom I have much respect, for his knowledge and experience are wide, his standards high, his judgement is sound and his taste impeccable. I think you will thoroughly enjoy his vivid account of the life and times of a remarkable building. I know I shall … again and again.

Leslie Sands

Acknowledgements

My sincere thanks to the scores of people I have met and interviewed over the years in connection with the Bradford Alhambra. All in some way were to contribute to this book, although neither I nor they were aware of it at the time. My particular gratitude to Queenie Roma, G. William Kershaw, Terry Quinn, Bernard Mitchell, Robin Derham, Brian Baines and John Martin. My biggest debt is to the late Charlie Handby and to Rowland Hill who in my youth both tutored me in the ways of the theatre. To them especially I am immensely grateful. Finally, my thanks to Bradford Libraries and Information Service for undertaking the publication of this book, and in particular to Reference Librarian, Bob Duckett, who compiled the index and saw to the final editing.

for

Rowland Hill

The Background

On Thursday evening, October 30th 1986, at the official reopening of the beautifully refurbished Alhambra Theatre, Bradford, Monsieur Jacques Delours, president of the Commission of the European Communities, told a glittering gathering that the Alhambra was now a little part of Europe.

It gave him joy to say it and the assembly was delighted to hear it. Delighted too, I'm sure, was the EEC itself, for in a spirit of growing European fellowship it had contributed more than £2 million towards the £8.2 millions the improvements had cost.

The occasion was proof that the EEC was prepared to help those who helped themselves. Yet, hopefully more important in the long run, it was a magnificent example of Bradford's determination to overcome, no matter how many economic hurdles, the problems of the technological revolution and to win back universal esteem for a great city in which first-rate theatre should play a prominent part, as it had done in the past.

The city that gave the world J. B. Priestley, Frederick Delius, David Hockney and John Braine, suffered severely when the employment crisis hardened but with a campaign against knee-buckling it insisted that *Bradford's Bouncing Back.*

This rallying cry was taken up, not only by citizens whose Bradford ancestry went back generations, but also by the huge cosmopolitan population which had emerged in Bradford since the second world war. Tourism too became a quickly expanding Bradford industry and there were to be countless visitors who discovered that, as the posters boasted, Bradford really is *A Surprising Place.*

One early sign of the city's re-emergence as an important cultural centre was the Government's decision to establish the National Museum of Photography, Film and Television there, while the famous old concert hall, St. George's, was lovingly renovated and improved after a serious fire.

While retaining and treasuring some of the best of its old buildings, like the Wool Exchange and the Victorian edifices of the Little Germany quarter, redesigned Bradford has scores of imposing new buildings and dozens of pleasant thoroughfares, all complemented by expanses of greenery.

The refurbished Alhambra, immediately appreciated as a sparkling jewel of the city, is in a section which is being developed as Bradford's own West End, an area where theatregoers will find many additional attractions including bistros, bars and night-spots.

The area has a vastly different aspect from that familiar to Bradfordians just before the 1914-18 war, when the Alhambra was built. The city then was a West Riding wool town to its loom-clattering core. Grimy in the extreme, its mill masters had good reason to coin the saying: "Where there's muck, there's brass".

One of the least salubrious areas of the city centre was a triangular shaped wilderness, lined by black warehouses and an aged belching brewery, known as the Morley Street Waste.

Few could have foreseen that this would provide the site for one of the most opulent and glamorous theatres of the North and one which would ultimately survive all the other theatres then flourishing in Bradford.

The Alhambra, as it was to be called, was a romantic evocation of the Alhambra palace in Granada, Spain, and its three domes became instantly synonymous with first-class entertainment. Today, after many ebbs and flows of box-office fortune, they shine brighter than ever. They stand proudly as Bradford's Domes of Delight, and as an enduring monument to the man whose vision and initiative made it possible — Francis Laidler.

Francis Laidler
" … the man whose vision and initiative made it possible."

Francis Laidler

Shrewd, dapper, slightly vain, quietly but relentlessly ambitious. Courteous, secretive, canny, even stingy with his brass, yet occasionally extremely generous. A man who loved children dearly, a dreamer who magically brought fairy tales to life, but still a dogmatic boss who expected loyalty. A slave to work until his late years, an opponent of crudity and of any suggestion of bad taste (apart from one notable exception) and a man passionate in the ardour of marital relationships. Above all, a dedicated and great impresario to the tips of his delicate fingers. This, in its complicated totality, was Francis Laidler.

During his earlier life, however, no-one could have guessed he was destined to bring theatrical delight, not only to the people of Bradford, but to those of London's West End and numerous provincial cities. As for the crown of the King of Pantomime, which eventually was to be his, not even he could have had a visionary's foresight of it.

Laidler was already thirty-five when, in 1902, he became associated with the stage. Until then he had all the appearance and prospects of a rising middle-class businessman. Noting his softly-spoken self-assurance and seeing him in one of those immaculately tailored suits he favoured throughout his life, you could have thought him the chief clerk of a bank, a successful accountant or an executive in the wool trade. Nevertheless, half a century later, when he died on the day before his 88th birthday, Francis Laidler was one of Britain's best-known and most respected men of the theatre, climbing to his pre-eminent position entirely through his own abilities and initiative.

He was born at Thornaby-on-Tees on January 7th 1867, the son of a doctor, Joseph Laidler M.R.C.S., L.S.A. He spent his schooldays at Wharfedale College, Boston Spa, and at the Darlington Grammar School. The family hoped that, like his father, he would be attracted to the medical profession, but an early budding of his business acumen pointed him in a different direction.

It took him to Stokesley where he was apprenticed in the service of the National Provincial Bank of England. The then North Riding town had many rural charms and there, in the springtime of his life, and with spring blossoms all around him, young Francis met, courted and, at twenty-one in February 1888, placed a wedding-ring on the finger of Miss Annie Unthank — *a bonnie Stokesley lass*. They were to have four daughters.

Rustic air is sweet to breathe. Nevertheless it wasn't long before Francis decided that in Stokesley there were far too few opportunities for his commercial and administrative flair. "Never heed, therefore," he said to himself, "the sooty murk and the acrid smell of greasy fleeces." It was off to Bradford to accept a promising position in the clerical department of one of the wool trade's leading houses.

After a fruitful period at Parker, Hodgson and Co., Francis moved to J. S. McLaren and Co., before being appointed secretary at Hammond's Bradford Brewery Company, an old and much esteemed concern in Manchester Road. During the later period of his seven years' service there he made considerable advancement and was finally promoted to management. Each of his job changes since leaving Stokesley had brought a higher salary and a more elevated position.

In spite of his success, however, something must have been lacking in his working life; or was it that he cherished theatrical ambitions he never spoke about or barely recognised himself? Why else should he have been drawn to the Prince's Theatre at the bottom of Bradford's Little Horton Lane?

The trading records of the Prince's would have put off nearly everyone who had any business sense. Although the theatre had been rebuilt after a disastrous fire in 1873, and had been reopened in 1879 by Alfred David of Sunderland, its existence had been precarious for years — so much so that locals came to call it the Folly Theatre. For one period during its many vicissitudes it had even been used as a Salvation Army barracks.

But it was at the Prince's in 1902 that Francis Laidler went into proprietorial partnership with its then leaseholder, Walter J. Piper, the son-in-law of Walter Reynolds who, as well as owning the Prince's, owned the Leeds Theatre Royal, (now, like the Prince's, demolished).

The proposal was that while Piper, who was also general manager, concentrated on the production side of the Prince's, Laidler should take charge of its financial affairs and, not unnaturally, the bars.

But the partnership, under whose auspices the first performance was given on September 8th 1902, was doomed. Within six months Walter Piper died and Francis Laidler, who was still manager of Hammond's Brewery, which provided him with lucrative security, was faced with the crucial problem of which path to take: should he turn his back on the theatre, or should he give up his brewery job and risk his chances at the Prince's?

He risked it. In early 1903 Laidler gave up his secure employment with the brewery to operate full-time as proprietor and manager of the Bradford Prince's Theatre, but with so little experience of theatre administration that it would not have surprised anyone had he gone bankrupt almost immediately.

At the very start fate seemed against him. Only weeks before he died, Walter Piper had insured his new partner Laidler for £1,000 — a huge sum in those days when you consider that only eleven years later the cost of building the 1914 Alhambra was less than £20,000. The insurance company then sent a young representative to urge Francis to take out a similar policy for his partner. Laidler, out of delicacy, refused. Later the young insurance man admitted that had a more experienced agent been sent, Mr. Laidler might have been induced to overcome his scruples and the company would have been losers by £1,000. That money would have been a valuable safety-net for Laidler as he stepped the high-wire of controlling the Prince's, but he appears never to have felt a moment's regret.

3

Francis Laidler had one bright star guiding him, though, and it transpired to be an inspiring one. Had it not appeared, the whole story of Bradford theatre might have been very different with the likelihood that the Alhambra would never have been built.

That guiding star was in the shape of a pantomime. With his death only weeks away, Walter Piper, together with Francis Laidler, advertised that the Prince's first Christmas attraction under their partnership would be the pantomime, *Red Riding Hood.* Starring Gracie Graham, Fanny Harris, Percy Curry, Guy Drury and Teddy Gibbs, it made a big impression on the audience, but an even bigger one on Francis Laidler.

Quite simply, he was enraptured. Not only by that particular pantomime, but by the sheer magic of a form of entertainment which so involved and delighted the families who flocked to see it. He instantly foresaw that if he could produce a really good panto every year, it would bring in enough money to make the presentation of other stage ventures far less worrying. And so it proved, for during the next half-century the city and then the entire country acclaimed Laidler's remarkable mastery of the form until they finally recognised him as the undisputed King of Pantomime.

What is more, Laidler never truly needed to offset losses of any consequence on his non-panto production enterprises. Theatrically, he proved to have a God-given instinct which others — particularly those with bank managers knocking at the door — must have marvelled at.

He had not been in management long, for instance, when he brought the great Mrs. Patrick Campbell on a flying visit to the Prince's when she was at the very apex of her career. He also brought such Drury Lane productions as *Ben Hur, The Hope* and *The Whip* to the same theatre with the intention of elevating it to No. 1 touring status. Although this, while the Bradford Theatre Royal was still thriving, was never to be fully attained, Laidler considerably raised the image of the Prince's where the quality of its melodramas soon became widely admired.

It wasn't long either before Laidler further developed his undertakings by "entering upon touring business of extensive and modern character". One early success in this field was his production of the musical comedy, *The Pride of Byzantia,* which I note "went down particularly well at the Stoke Hippodrome".

All this while, however, Laidler was becoming more and more attracted towards Variety. The days were numbered, therefore, for that ugly waste land at the bottom of Morley Street.

Early Bradford Theatres

Today the Alhambra is Bradford's only full-time professional theatre. We shouldn't forget, however, that in 1912, when Francis Laidler decided to build on the Morley Street Waste, the city's and the West Riding's theatre scene was greatly different. The colossal upsurge of the cinema had not yet arrived and a night out at a live show was still the public's favourite form of relaxation.

Laidler gauged it brilliantly when he sensed a growing public desire for up-to-the-minute Variety in the comfortable, even glamorous, surroundings of the plush velvet and gilt of the Palaces, Empires and Hippodromes pioneered by Oswald Stoll and Edward Moss. Others, with less perception, must have thought him mad. Surely, they insisted, there were sufficient theatres in the area already?

The Empire Music Hall in Great Horton Road was almost opposite the present stage door of the Alhambra. Built by a syndicate of local businessmen and later operated

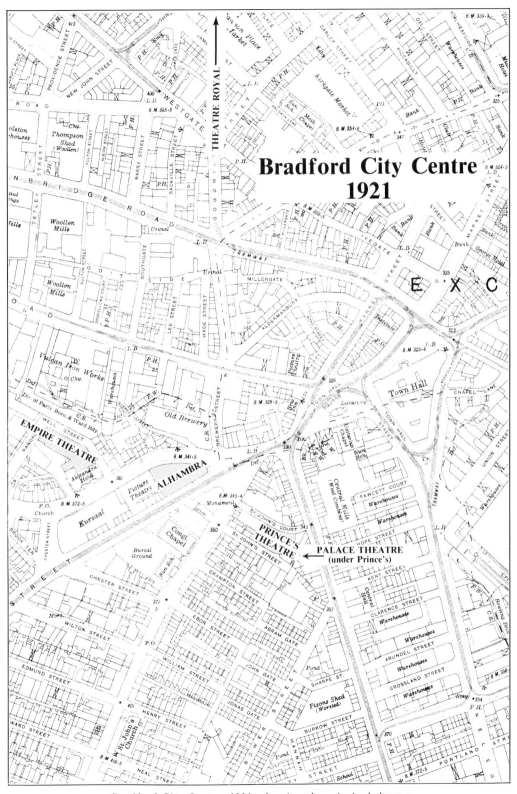

Bradford City Centre, 1921, showing the principal theatres

by Moss Empires, it had opened in 1889 and still, in 1912, featured many famous entertainers. Only two years previously, in 1910, a young comic had made a big impression in a Fred Karno sketch called *Jimmy the Fearless.* He was a Londoner named Charles Chaplin and, like another young favourite with the Bradford audience (an Ulverston lad called Stan Laurel), he was destined for California and worldwide film fame. To take a similar path after treading the Empire boards was a young comedy juggler called W. C. Fields. After its stage was destroyed by fire in 1917 the Empire was turned into a cinema.

The Palace Theatre in Manchester Road, (opened in 1875 and closed in 1938), had its ups and downs admittedly, and for a time was frowned upon by the more respectable citizens because of its "naughty" *Promenade.* But generally there had been vigorous support for its versatile Music Hall style bills. Many a future star began at the Palace (male impersonator Hetty King for example), and a few former stars found themselves middle of its bill — on their way down.

The Theatre Royal in Manningham Lane, now sorrowfully derelict, was launched in 1864 and became a cinema in 1921. Although it had its own fine pantomime tradition, it was principally the venue for No. 1 tours by West End "legitimate theatre" successes. It will always have a place in theatrical history, for it was at the Theatre Royal, on Friday, October 13th 1905, that Sir Henry Irving, Britain's first theatrical knight, gave his final performance before collapsing and dying in the foyer of the nearby Midland Hotel in Cheapside. He had been appearing in Tennyson's *Becket* and his very last line was, prophetically, "Into thy hands O Lord; into thy hands!" Next day the whole nation heard the news and wept.

The Prince's Theatre opened in Little Horton Lane in 1876 and closed in 1961. Ostensibly, Laidler didn't need to be apprenhensive about his Alhambra having competition from his home of drama, melodrama and many of his own pantomimes, for he already controlled it. Nevertheless, it was extremely well patronised and there were some who predicted that he would be cutting his own throat by going into such close competition with himself. (Incidentally, the Prince's incorporated a feature which, as far as I can discover, was unique in that its stage was immediately above, and back to back, with the stage of the Palace, the two theatres facing in opposite directions. Many are the legends of visiting performers getting lost behind the scenes and stumbling into the wrong show in the wrong theatre!)

By 1912, when Francis Laidler decided to build his own Alhambra Theatre, even many older Bradfordians had forgotten that the city had once had another Alhambra.

It had opened in 1873 as a wooden circus building opposite a L.M.S. Railway bonding warehouse in Canal Road. It was soon acquired by a local stationer called William Morgan who converted it into the Alhambra Music Hall. It was advertised as "The Most Fashionable Promenade in Bradford", which was "Comfortably Heated by a Patent Process".

The prices of admittance are interesting. Those who wished to be really extravagant and take a box had to pay a shilling (5p), while the second seats and side boxes were sixpence (2½p). The pit, however, was advertised in fat type, which suggests it was the real stand-by. The price was threepence.

The Seward Brothers' benefit, printed large on a March 1874 playbill seems to have been a great affair. The special attraction was J. R. Johnson, *The Hero of the London Bridge,* who was the most famous swimmer of his day. Announced prominently too was Mr. Sam Garton who had residential rights to be considered a Bradfordian. Sam figured on the bill as S. Garton Stream, "The Favourite Comic and Motto Vocalist".

Sam Stream, or "The Flowing Stream" as he was also called, was well known to the music hall patrons of Bradford. In 1872, for example, he appeared at Pullan's Music

Hall, Brunswick Place, where Dan Leno and Blondin, *The Hero of Niagara,* helped make it celebrated.

Sam also appeared on the first bill of the first Moss music hall at Greenock where Sir Edward Moss started his managerial career under his father James Moss. Sam figured on that programme as Master Stream. He was then in his teens.

The life of Bradford's first Alhambra ended in 1875 when William Morgan left to take over the new Star Music Hall in Manchester Road. Morgan was an exceptional man. Born in 1829 he became proprietor of the original Bradford Prince's Theatre when it opened in 1876, but was made nearly penniless when two years later the building was destroyed by fire. But he picked himself up, brushed himself down and started all over again.

He was the first in the country to introduce Saturday night concerts; and could be found two or three years later managing Morecambe's Winter Gardens. In 1886 he bought a share, along with two other men, of the Scarborough Aquarium which he was later to turn into the highly successful People's Palace.

This is not the place to go into too many details, even if Bradford's theatre history is full of fascinating ones, like those about William Morgan. Two facts shouldn't be omitted, though — if only for the benefit of any young people unaware of them. First, what could be called Bradford's original theatre went into business in the first quarter of the nineteenth century in Sackville Street, off Sunbridge Road. It was no more than a converted barn, but the playbills proudly advertised it as the Bradford Theatre. It was commonly known as Thompson's Theatre, its occupier being L. S. Thompson who, legend informs us, was extremely popular.

Second, the city's first important permanent theatre was the Theatre Royal which opened in Duke Street, off Darley Street, in 1841. It did well for twenty years, but declined swiftly when the handsome Royal Alexandra Theatre in Manningham Lane opened in 1864. It was pulled down three years later and its name was taken over by the Manningham Lane building which became the Theatre Royal.

And the name of one of the men instrumental in giving Bradford its Manningham Lane Theatre Royal? Yes, it was William Morgan.

Genesis

The year 1912, when Francis Laidler decided to build the Bradford Alhambra, saw what was in many ways the apotheosis of variety entertainment in Britain. It had its roots in the coarser, earthier and often outright vulgar music hall of the late nineteenth century. But with the rapid expansion of the respectable Edwardian middle-classes a new type of family entertainment was developed. It was pioneered by two great impresarios, Oswald Stoll and Edward Moss who, like Francis Laidler, both deplored bad taste.

To accommodate this new form of entertainment Stoll and Moss both built throughout Britain a chain of palatial, innovative theatres of unprecedented luxury to replace the seedy taverns and small music halls of the eighteen eighties and nineties.

The triumph of the new-style Variety over the immorality of the old music halls was recognised on July 1st 1912, when the very first Royal Command Variety Performance was staged at the Palace Theatre, London, in the presence of King George V and Queen Mary. The Cinderella of the arts, as Stoll remarked, had finally gone to the ball.

This upsurge in the popularity of Variety, coupled with his own interest in it, may well have persuaded Francis Laidler that Bradford should have a theatre which would equal the grandeur of those on the Stoll and Moss circuits, and that if he didn't take immediate steps towards building it, somebody else would.

The first essential was to find a suitable site; and looking out of his window at the Prince's Theatre, his glance fell upon the eyesore of the Morley Street Waste. In that moment of inspiration he saw the building which was to be the Bradford Alhambra.

" ... his glance fell upon the eyesore of the Morley Street Waste."

That triangular piece of land was more than 1,500 square yards in extent and had been a left-over after Bradford Corporation had bought a large area for street improvement and the construction of a new highway. In 1897 the Corporation then sold it for nearly £8,000 to wool merchant William Horsfall Greenwood, who presumably wanted it for private development. But it was still a hideous eyesore when Laidler took a lease on it for ninety-eight years and six months.

The Alhambra was built from designs and under the supervision of Messrs. Chadwick and Watson of Leeds and the general contractor was Mr. J. T. Wright, also of Leeds. The fibrous plaster and decorators' work was by Messrs. F. DeJong and Co. Ltd. of London.

The word Alhambra is derived from the Arabic Kal'-at al hambra, which means *the red castle.* Although Laidler's new theatre may have owed something in inspiration to the great citadel and palace built by the Moorish kings of the 13th century, a greater influence in practical terms was the Alhambra Theatre and music hall in London's Leicester Square, built on a site now occupied by the Odeon Cinema. Opened in 1858 it was designed entirely in the Moorish style and, unlike the Bradford Alhambra, the exotic motifs of Islam extended into the auditorium.

Faced externally with white terra-cotta, the Bradford Alhambra was a two-tier building in advance of its time. The accommodation consisted of orchestra stalls and pit stalls on the ground floor, dress circle and eight boxes on the first tier and a large balcony on the second tier. The total seating capacity was nearly 1,800, later reduced to 1,650. There were wide promenades behind the pit stalls, the dress circle and balcony, while another much praised feature was the height of the pit stalls ceiling, which made the pit stalls spacious and lofty.

Other striking features were the width of the stage (35ft.) and the tip-up seating of the pit which, to most people's amazement, was upholstered just as comfortably as the seats in the orchestra stalls and dress circle. What's more, the whole of the ground floor was covered from the orchestra rail to the back wall with thick, rich and specially manufactured carpet.

The most remarkable amenity, however, was that the theatre, erected on the cantilever principle, had no auditorium pillars to obstruct the view. Every part of the stage could be seen from every seat in the house.

The main entrance was at the front circular corner of the building and the walls of the entrance had tiled dados. Above, the walls and ceilings were daintily decorated with ornamental plaster, panels and moulding. From the main staircase there was access to the dress circle, while the orchestra stalls were reached from the main entrance hall on the ground floor, through a doorway, down three steps only and through the pit stalls. This mode of easy entrance into the orchestra stalls was quite new to the provinces. The entrance to the pit stalls and balcony was in Morley Street, separate from the main entrance on the corner.

The theatre was heated by low pressure hot water and ventilated by electric extraction fans. It was brightly illuminated by electricity and there was gas in all corridors and exits in case the electric current failed.

Although the auditorium has for long now suggested to us the splendour of a typical Edwardian theatre, it was actually the Louis XVI style which was emulated by many of the internal decorations. This was particularly true of the attractive fibrous plaster ornamentation on the proscenium front and on the boxes. Over the years the main colour of the stage curtain and the furnishings has remained red or blue (and for one period red and blue were mixed).

The original scenery was painted by the best scenic artists of the day, Mr. G. Sackmann and Mr. G. R. Hersley of London, and Messrs. Dodsworth and Spencer of Bradford. Although I haven't been able to confirm it, I suspect it was one or more of those talented artists who painted the very impressive semi-circular mural high above the proscenium frame, and which has now been restored.

Today we must consider the backstage facilities of the 1914 Alhambra sadly inadequate, but at a time when most managements directed all their efforts to getting "bums on seats", and had lesser regard for the needs of the performers, they were thought to be very progressive.

Artists at the Alhambra considered themselves very well looked after: there were no less than eleven dressing rooms, each supplied with hot and cold water, and fitted with gas and electric light. On each level of dressing rooms there was a separate auxiliary emergency exit — not at all common then.

Of greater significance to the artists, perhaps, was the notice attached to each dressing room door. It read: "Please do not ask the Management for complimentary tickets for your friends. If your friends will not pay to see you, why should the public?"

The Alhambra Opens

The official opening of the Alhambra was scheduled for Wednesday, March 18th 1914, but although the theatre had been built at remarkable speed, the management was still catching its breath after a last-minute rush when it was feared that it would not be completed in time.

Walter Havers, the Alhambra's first manager (he had previously been manager of the Keighley Hippodrome), recalled that "In Bradford I found the new building a hive of industry with Italians busily engaged on the tessellated marble work which was to make the foyer of the theatre so attractive, and countless workmen engaged on various jobs.

"I realised it was to be a race against time if the theatre was to be ready for the opening on the date selected, for the builders and decorators were a long way behind schedule.

"A few days before the advertised time it looked extremely doubtful if the theatre could possibly open, but by a lot of persuasion of one sort or another we got rid of the workmen on the eve preceding the opening, although they left behind a good deal of rubbish for us to clear.

"This necessitated the engagement of a small army of cleaners and all through the night they worked like Trojans. Nat Hepworth, the Alhambra secretary, and I worked side by side with cleaners with buckets, brushes and soap; and when Mr. Laidler came on the scene at an early hour to see how things were progressing, he insisted that we should all go across to the Great Northern Hotel (now the Victoria Hotel) for a well-earned breakfast."

The Bradford Alhambra Theatre shown in its opening week, 1914

In the event the Alhambra Theatre was officially opened on schedule. The actual ceremony was very quietly performed at 2 p.m. on March 18th 1914 by Mrs Annie Laidler, wife of Francis who was by now the proud Managing Director of the Alhambra Company. To witness the historic event a small assembly of friends and colleagues had gathered at the main entrance.

Mr. William Watson of Chadwick and Watson, the architects, introduced Mrs. Laidler and explained that her recent ill-health had made it necessary that the opening should be carried out in an informal and quiet way.

Little Miss Olive Laidler, one of four sisters, then handed her mother a golden key with which Mrs. Laidler unlocked one of the doors. All present entered and made their way to a circle buffet where a toast was drunk to the future prosperity of the Alhambra. After this they were shown round the building, which had been decorated with flowers. "This seemed in the circumstances," jested one journalist, "almost like the painting of the lily and the guilding of refined gold".

By 3 p.m. a large number of important guests had arrived to inspect the then ultra-modern wonders of the new theatre. They were headed by the Lord Mayor and Lady Mayoress (Alderman and Mrs. John Arnold) and included many civic representatives and prominent citizens who were given afternoon tea to the music of an orchestra directed by Geoffrey W. Jackson.

The stage curtain then went up to reveal, in a striking stage setting, and seated in a semi-circle, many of those most closely associated with the Alhambra venture. Councillor Dr. David Walker, chairman of the occasion, congratulated Mr. Laidler on the speed of the Alhambra's completion.

Francis Laidler emphasised that in his opinion the really important matter was not the Alhambra building itself, but that the public should have "a clear and distinct understanding that they were going to have the best of all Variety talents to occupy the Alhambra stage".

With this in view he had approached Walter De Freece (later Sir Walter), Managing Director of the Variety Theatres Control company, to ask him to join him in the booking of quality artists. De Freece, who was married to the greatest of all male impersonators, Vesta Tilley, had agreed.

One man on stage in the semi-circle of notabilities must have been worried by the determination of Laidler and De Freece to succeed so starrily at the Alhambra — even if he didn't lose his calm smile. He was Percival Craig, the manager of the nearby Empire Theatre. With dignity he got to his feet and appealed to the public to dip a little deeper into their pockets and purses so that they could patronise *both* the Empire and the Alhambra.

When, after this plea, he and Laidler shook hands, there was loud applause from the auditorium. What was really going on in the minds of the two men, though, we can only guess.

First Shows

Five days after its official launching the Alhambra opened its doors to the general public at 6.30 p.m. on Monday, March 23rd 1914. On the afternoon of that day, however, there had been a special matinee when artists from the first week's show entertained an audience which, according to Walter Havers, included "everybody of note in Bradford and a number of stage celebrities from all parts of the country."

From the beginning, the Alhambra operated as a twice-nightly theatre, with shows at 6.50 and 9 p.m. Prices were: Boxes 15s. (75p.) and 10s. (50p.) with single seats at 2s. 6d. (12½p.); orchestra stalls 1s. 6d. (7½p.); dress circle 1s. (5p.); pit stalls 9d. (4p. approximately). The advance booking office was open from 9 a.m. to 9 p.m. and there were no fees payable for reserving tickets in advance.

Walter Havers remarked on a novelty which within days had the Variety world talking excitedly: "There were no early doors and every seat — no matter the price — was bookable, thus avoiding the necessity of queuing. It was a startling innovation that was to be widely copied."

Comics were to become an outstanding characteristic of Variety. Yet from the start the Alhambra patrons made it clear they were not going to throw their hats in the air just because of this.

Noted Mr. Havers: "The attitude of the audiences was apparently: 'Go on, now, Make us laugh — if tha can!' And generally speaking they did not. To try to remedy this

World Events in 1914

- Tarzan of The Apes, first of the Tarzan books by Edgar Rice Burroughs, published.

- Beniamino Gigli, the Italian tenor, made debut in La Gioconda.

- Robert H. Goddard, of America, undertook practical experiments with rockets.

- Philosopher Bertrand Russell published *Our Knowledge of The External World*.

- Irish Parliament restored by Irish Home Rule Act.

- Carson formed Ulster volunteers to oppose integration with South Ireland.

- Cyprus and Egypt became British protectorates.

- War declared on August 4th.

- Battles of the Marne and Mons began.

- Britain made its first one-seater fighter aircraft.

- First Zeppelin raid.

- Bradford-born Frederick Delius composed the orchestral North Country Sketches.

- Picasso created the cubist painting *The Small Table*.

- *Rossignol,* a ballet by Stravinsky, composed.

- *Graf Spee's* squadron destroyed at Falklands.

- The Panama Canal was completed.

Bradford Events in 1914

- January 2nd, North of England Education Conference in Bradford.
- January 28th, Marsh Gas explosions in Lumb Lane.
- February 10th, Bradford City Council buys Royal Infirmary for £100,000.
- March 5th, Two prisoners escape from Town Hall Cells.
- March 14th, Mr. Winston Churchill, First Lord, speaks at St. George's Hall.
- March 18th, Alhambra Theatre opened by Mrs. Francis Laidler.
- April 14th, Mr. F. W. Jowett M.P. elected chairman of the Independent Labour Party, Bradford.
- May 29th, Two Bradford men among 1,024 lives lost when *Empress of Ireland* wrecked.
- June 6th, Chief Scout Baden-Powell reviews Bradford Boy Scouts.
- August 4th, War declared.
- August 6th, Lord Mayor's War Relief Fund inaugurated.
- August 10th, Bradford Territorials left for war duty at Selby.
- September 16th, Great recruiting campaign starts locally.
- October 27th, First party of wounded soldiers brought to Bradford (50 of them).
- November 6th, Lights in shops lowered and railway carriage blinds drawn.
- December 16th, Bradford people in German bombardment of Scarborough.

we inserted a notice in the programme asking the audience kindly to applaud because it encouraged the artists. But to no avail. I know now why Bradford was known as the comedian's grave.''

One comedian who would have agreed was Lancashire's George Formby (father of the ukelele-playing funster of the same name), who had most other audiences in the land in fits of laughter with his characterisation of a woman-dominated, helpless wimp.

One day Walter Havers was talking to George outside the Alhambra when the comedian commented on the coolness of the Bradford audiences. Then, glancing up at the domes of the new theatre, which were gleaming bright in the sun, he remarked: "Anyway, yon's a fine tombstone for a comic!"

The first performer to be heard at the Alhambra "baptised" the building some time before it opened. Her name was Clarice May and she was the famous principal boy, with the equally famous figure, in the Leeds Theatre Royal pantomime, *Aladdin*. She was being shown over the new building and was asked to try its acoustics from the stage — with very satisfactory results.

By coincidence it was another principal boy who actually opened the proceedings at the first public show on that evening of March 23rd 1914. She was Alice Wyatt who, until a few days before, had been starring in *Robinson Crusoe* for Francis Laidler at the Prince's Theatre. (The cast also included the Yeadon-born comic Sydney Howard, Mamie Watson and Leslie Barker.)

Miss Wyatt provided the first Alhambra item by singing the National Anthem. An observer commented: "She was so overcome by the importance of the occasion that many people thought she would never get through it, though she quickly recovered".

This first programme was shared by a group of individual "turns" and a revue which took up half the programme. Revue was then rapidly becoming a principal feature of many variety bills. The one at the Alhambra had been anticipated with much excitement by Bradfordians, to whom this type of entertainment was completely novel.

On Tuesday, March 24th, a Bradford reviewer wrote: "Appropriately enough the new Alhambra provides for its opening week a distinct novelty as the principal item. Wylie and Tate's *A Year in an Hour* is a real revue at last".

Advertised as being from the London Palladium and Oxford Music Hall, *A Year in an Hour* was a series of sketches spread over the seasons and involved an elderly couple in search of peace and quiet. "Their failure to find them," wrote the same reviewer, "may be taken as a commentary on modern life, and that is just one instance of the abundant topicalities which do, for once, justify the title of Revue."

A prominent name on the remainder of the first-night programme was that of Nellie Wallace, billed as "The Female Dan Leno" and "The Essence of Eccentricity". In her tatty feather boa, woolly jumper and silly little hat, she was superb with her timing and delivery of comic songs.

Other "turns" on the bill included Royal and Rejane (The Men With Tangled Feet, otherwise known as Two Men, Two Chairs and Some Dancing) and the acrobatic Benedetti Brothers (Music Mixed With Quaintness Of Comedy), all of whom were warmly received.

Our reviewer was less impressed, though, when he noted: "The orchestra did not appear to have found itself accompanistically and as its individual item was that most hackneyed of all music hall classicalism, the *William Tell* overture, one may defer judgement."

More charitably he concluded: "Since this is the first week, a word of praise should be given to the attendants who are smart in appearance and unwaveringly amiable.

"It may be added that quite the best attraction at the Alhambra this week is — the Alhambra!"

Branching Out

When the Alhambra opened, Bradford still languished in a post-Edwardian summertime of confidence, rugged vitality and nonconformist principles. There were few signs that the existing class structure and established values could be shaken; and the chapel, the boss's big house and the Town Hall still commanded cap-doffing respect. Besides, with its black forest of mill chimneys, wasn't Bradford, in spite of its smokey, sooty grime, the envy of the industrial world?

Nevertheless, before the year was out the horrendous carnage of the first World War was to spell the end of much Bradfordian self-assurance. News of death stalked every street, and the anguish and misery had hardly been eased by the trumpets of victory before the spectre of mass unemployment loomed.

Almost in a twinkling then, Francis Laidler's theatre, which, with its exotic Moorish domes, had started out as an architectural oddity (at least to no-messing West Riding folk), became a temple of comfort where, communally, the people of Bradford could find blessed escape from the hardships and disappointments of their traumatically changed existence.

They grew to love their Alhambra dearly, and those people seventy years later who (understandable though it was) condemned many of the theatre's features as badly antiquated, should be reminded that during its early years the Bradford Alhambra was a modern marvel to the thousands whose lives it brightened.

The Alhambra, however, was far from being Francis Laidler's sole enterprise. It is perhaps the right moment therefore to consider some of his other achievements. In 1909, for example, he had leased from Walter Reynolds the Theatre Royal, Leeds, and in 1913 he took control of the Keighley Hippodrome.

For many years the Leeds Theatre Royal was to share with the Alhambra the honour of being a principal platform for Laidler pantomimes. Indeed, it was at the Theatre Royal in 1945 that one of his productions, *Humpty, Dumpty,* broke the record for the longest ever run in England by a panto — twenty-two astonishing weeks.

As well as housing pantomime, the Theatre Royal was frequently to be the home of resident repertory companies, as was the Bradford Prince's where the Terence Byron Company and the Harry Hanson Court Players were favourites, the latter companies remaining popular until well into the 1950's.

Not too long after the 1914-18 war, when things looked as if they might yet get back to normal, Laidler floated Yorkshire Theatres Limited, a company whose main assets were the Alhambra, the Leeds Theatre Royal and the Keighley Hippodrome — plus an interest in Francis's flourishing pantomimes.

In 1916, with the Alhambra an ever-increasing success, Laidler was approached by Frank Allen, Managing Director of Moss Empires Ltd., the country's most respected and effective Variety organisation. Allen had the idea of coming to an arrangement to restrict competition between the Alhambra and the nearby Bradford Empire in Great Horton Road — a competition which was working to the detriment of the Empire, which was operated by Moss Empires.

Following this meeting Moss Empires became the booking agents for the Alhambra and remained so for more than forty years. Before the arrangement was terminated in 1959, when the Alhambra management itself took over the booking of artists, almost every big-name variety performer had been booked by Moss Empires to appear at the Alhambra.

The arrangement was launched by a display advertisement in *The Yorkshire Observer* and read: "Today, Monday, May 1st 1916, the Bradford Alhambra Theatre of Varieties Ltd. is amalgamated with Moss Empires Ltd., the World's Greatest Amusement Caterers, and the programmes at Bradford's Palatial Variety Theatre in Victoria Square are now provided by Moss Empires Ltd. Mr. Frank Allen, the Managing Director of Moss Empires Ltd., hopes that his Bradford Empire patrons will support the Bradford Alhambra, of which he is joint director with Mr. Francis Laidler''.

Even with that 1916 arrangement, however, and even though the Empire was reseated, redecorated and, after a short closure for structural alterations, renamed the Empire Theatre and Opera House, the Empire's fortunes hardly improved. It was agreed, therefore, that Laidler could take over its lease for his pet scheme of trying to make it a number one once-nightly theatre — a theatre similar to the Bradford Theatre Royal in the days before leaseholder John Hart took control of the Grand Theatre, Leeds, as well. Hart soon relinquished the lease of the Theatre Royal and its future hung in the balance.

Fate, unfortunately, was to play an unwelcome part at the Empire, for on November 21st 1917, the building was severely damaged and its roof structure destroyed after a fire broke out in the 'gods'. Ironically, or perhaps, prophetically, the title of that night's show was *Ye Gods.*

Theatre experts agreed that the fire, when added to other problems, had made the Empire's situation desperate. Suitable shows had become even scarcer because of the war, and with the Alhambra continuing to attract the bulk of the city's light entertainment lovers, it was common sense to call it a day. Consequently, before 1917 was out, the Empire was sub-let for twenty-one years to Gaumont-British to run as a cinema. When this sub-lease ran out in 1938 it was not renewed by Gaumont-British because of their interest in the huge 3,300 seater New Victoria Cinema (now the Odeon), which had opened in 1930. (Incidentally, after its first name change to the Gaumont, the New Victoria was to be the setting for some famous Bradford concerts by the Beatles and the Rolling Stones.)

Because Gaumont-British did not renew the sub-lease, the Empire was then sub-let to various private managements which ran it as a cinema until a fire in January, 1952. A year or two previously the by then Hammonds United Breweries Limited had bought the freehold from Moss Empires Limited. They decided not to rebuild as a cinema and instead converted the building into an extension of the Alexandra Hotel.

On June 3rd 1920, to the great surprise of the public, if not to managements, the Bradford Theatre Royal was offered for sale by auction. For more than half a century it had been an important date in the diaries of top touring companies and Bradfordians cherished it. "What's up?" they asked themselves in some perplexity. Had they but known it, the prime cause for the auction was the decision by John Hart, its Lessee, to take control of the Leeds Grand.

Before that Bradford had been getting better bookings than Leeds, but when Hart had the monopoly in both towns he took his big attractions to the Grand because of its greater capacity, and Bradford suffered as a result. The favouring of Leeds unfortunately took hold so firmly that it became a tradition — a tradition only now certain of being broken because of the superb and superior facilities of Bradford's "new" Alhambra.

The successful bidder at the 1920 Theatre Royal auction was Francis Laidler, who not only bought a theatre but also bought much unfair criticism, some of it bordering on the slanderous. It accused him of buying the Royal for the sole purpose of closing it as a theatre and thus removing competition. This just was not true. Laidler's intention had been to carry on the splendid traditions of the place, even if most of those who had bid against him did intend turning the place into a cinema.

When Laidler came into possession, however, the Royal's capacity was too small to meet the enormous rise in the cost of productions which the war had brought about.

Nor was there any chance of enlarging the auditorium except by encroaching on the stage, and he reluctantly gave up the idea.

So, sorrowfully, after little more than a year's ownership, he formed a company called Bradford Theatre Royal Picture House Limited and subsequently sold it. Theatre was his life and he had no desire to get involved in cinema management. The sale of the Theatre Royal was probably the saddest decision Francis Laidler ever had to make.

The Alhambra's Early Years

In 1916 John Hart handed over the lease of the Theatre Royal to Nathaniel Hepworth, the same Nat Hepworth who was the Alhambra's first secretary. He found business at the Royal hard going and the 1920 auction was the outcome.

During Nat's first Theatre Royal night, a young Bradford lad was shouting "Five minutes please" down the Alhambra corridors to the artists preparing to go on stage. He was fifteen years old and already he had worked a year as the Alhambra's much-liked call-boy. When I last spoke to him in June 1986 he was a lively eighty-five year-old William Kershaw, living in King's Road, Bradford. From him came reminiscences about the Alhambra which not only brought back the flavour of the theatre's beginnings, but captured memorably the first world war atmosphere:

"At the Alhambra," he remembered, "I called and ran small errands for well-known people like Vesta Tilley, Harry Lauder, Hetty King, George Formby Senior and Florrie Forde — names that still ring a bell, even for generations who never knew them.

"The call-boy's job was bright, colourful and interesting, though even to a carefree young teenager like me, the shadow of the war was never far away. Not that we people at home had the slightest conception of the extent of the casualties we were sustaining in France.

"In England the pick of our manhood was responding to Kitchener's stern call. One by one the young men were leaving the Alhambra to don khaki, encouraged by some of the older ones who 'only wished they were ten years younger', or by glamorous young women appearing at the theatre who 'didn't want to lose them, but thought they ought to go'. Patriotic and recruiting songs were the order of the day. In most shows some charmer would sing:

'On Monday I walk out with a soldier,
On Tuesday I walk out with a tar ...' taking the arm of a 'super'
appropriately costumed at each line. On some occasions the third line, 'On Wednesday I'm out with a baby Boy Scout', was my cue to step out of the prompt entrance in Scout uniform, take the young lady's arm and stroll across the stage to join the other favoured partners.

"Those were also the days of the great illusionists. Names like Lafayette, David Devant, Oswald Williams and Chung Ling Soo pulled in the crowds. They too participated in the prevailing patriotic fervour. Oswald Williams did a trick which he called *The House That John Bull Built*. In this piece of magic I, among others, had the experience of being materialised out of thin air. For this illusion he used a lath and canvas cottage, raised up on stilts from the stage.

"Closing the doors of this obviously empty house, he announced: 'This is the house that John Bull built.' After a slight pause he reopened the doors with a dramatic gesture and proclaimed: 'This is the treasure that lay in the house that Jack built' and there, behold, stood myself as a miniature Australian trooper and two other boys representing Canada and New Zealand.

"Stepping down, we marched to the side of the stage and stood at attention. Few of

A page from the Manager's Report Book. Lilly Langtry's was "a delightful sketch", but Billy Simpson's was "A dreadful turn!"

ALHAMBRA,

Managing Director

Manager's Report.

Names of Artistes in Order of Merit	Business	How Received by Audience	Manager's Opinion (To be expressed Fully, but Concisely)
Staverdale Quintette	Instrumentalists	Very Well	Good turn. Audience strictly quiet throughout. Scored good encore
Mrs Langtry	Sketch	Very well	A delightful sketch much enjoyed by audience
Clown Barker	Animal Circus	Very well	A clever act. Good last turn
Bolton & Delmore	Comedy Sketch	Fairly Well	Rather disappointing considering he is a Bradford Panto Favorite
Scott Gibson	Sketch Comedian	Well	First part was quite good. Second song dropped success of first part.
Walter Gray	Juggler	Fair	Fairly good first turn
Maud Esmond	Vocal Comedienne	Not very well	Turn too long.
Billy Simpson	Character Artiste	Badly	A dreadful turn.

23 March 1915

18

BRADFORD.

FRANCIS LAIDLER.

Week commencing _22ᵈ March_ _1915_

Estimated Value of Each Turn		Worth Re-booking for Here ?	Opposition Entertainments	Business Done There	General Remarks : State of Trade Coming Local Events, Suggestions
1 —Value to House in regard to Pleasing Audience	2.—Value taking into consideration number in Act, Travelling, Subordinates Salaries, Scenery, Properties, &c.				Include herein any suggestion or fact in regard to a Turn to which attention should be drawn.
$27\frac{1}{2}$	$27\frac{1}{2}$	Yes	Theatre Royal "Country Girl"	Good	
Sharing	Terms	No.	Empire "Now we know"	Fair	
30	30	Yes	Princes "Melodrama"	Fair	
		Not appb	Palace "Gaston Chevalier"	Poor.	
10	10	No			
8	10	No.			
Nil	Nil	No.			
Nil	Nil	No			

Signature _____

MANAGER.

19

us had any doubts or misgivings about the position of the British Empire in the world, and to storms of applause Oswald Williams, in like manner, produced a stage full of representatives of that Empire and notabilities of all the Allies.

"On occasions, even greater celebrities than the usual stars of Variety made guest appearances at the Alhambra — Madame Sarah Bernhardt, for example. She played the role of a wounded French soldier in a short sketch. As she had unfortunately suffered the loss of a leg in reality, this part entailed no movement on the stage. What I thought of this seemingly incongruous role, I cannot clearly recall, but I do remember the distinct sense of occasion we all felt.

"But the one who received the greatest acclaim from the alleged undemonstrative Bradford audience was Grock, the great clown. It was said that he could give his act in every language of Europe. Never, either then, before or since, have I seen a performer get such vociferously enthusiastic applause as he did after each performance.

"Finlay Dunn, a popular entertainer at the piano, was a humourist and joker on and off the stage. He always ended his act with an impression of a mechanical piano. He would draw the edge of a penny rapidly along the keys, drop it on the end of the keyboard and proceed to rattle off a lively tune in a facile but mechanical fashion.

"I must explain that, when the stage manager dropped the 'tabs' at the end of the act, I had to run on to the stage just behind the fall of the curtain and grab the two halves to prevent them swinging apart again and so reveal the mundane activity that went on between the turns. Twice nightly, after doing this, I retrieved the penny from the piano unchallenged by the rest of the stage staff. At the second house, Saturday night, I noticed that he did it with a florin or half a crown. So did the stage manager. 'Never mind the tabs', he said to me, 'I'll look after them. You dash straight for the piano and get that two bob piece, or whatever it is'.

"This I did — and so did every single one of the stage hands! Whoever got the coin after the ensuing scuffle, it was never me. I noticed Finlay Dunn standing in the wings with a twinkle in his eye during this scrimmage.

"Meanwhile, our real war dragged on. Patriotic fervour was wearing a bit thin. The army was making increasing demands on our manpower and it was not unusual for male performers to wear, during their acts, the khaki armlet with the red crown to show that they had attested under the Lord Derby scheme.

"St. Luke's Hospital had been designated a war hospital and Red Cross trains from the south, filled with wounded soldiers, were frequent arrivals at Bradford's mainline terminals. Audiences at the Alhambra were liberally sprinkled with the lads in hospital blue, and with their white shirts and red ties they added a touch of colour to the Bradford scene. Despite their crutches, bandages and walking sticks, they were a cheerful bunch.

"Had we known the truth most of them were probably glad to have 'copped a blighty one', but there were many more acute cases at St. Luke's who had less reason for being cheerful.

"In that bright summer of 1918 I left the Alhambra and Bradford and when I returned (William Kershaw joined the 6th Batallion, West Yorkshire Regiment) the war was over''.

The Sunbeams

During the 1914-18 war Francis Laidler started a charming tradition which still flourishes at the Alhambra — although, incredibly, it was almost abandoned sixty or so years later when a pantomime production company worked at the theatre with no knowledge of the enterprises of the old "governor", as many of his staff used to call him. Fortunately they learned of the tradition in the nick of time and it was restored.

That tradition is the Sunbeams — dancing troups of little girls, recruited and auditioned locally, who annually added youthful high spirits to the Laidler pantomimes, during which they would often join in the comic capers.

Laidler selected the first team of Sunbeams for his 1917 pantomime, *Robin Hood,* at the Prince's Theatre, Bradford, and they were an immediate success with audiences. Bringing a ray of human sunshine to the darkness of the war years, they were adored not only by the audiences but by the panto's adult cast, including Lily Vine, Winnie Goodwin and Fred Walmsley, the "King of the Pierrots". When in 1930-31 Laidler switched his pantomimes from the Prince's to the Alhambra with a production of *Mother Goose* the Sunbeam tradition went with them.

Francis Laidler and The Sunbeams during panto preparations in the upstairs rehearsal room at the old Bradford Prince's Theatre

Over the years hundreds of little Yorkshire lasses spent excited weeks at the Alhambra or the Theatre Royal, Leeds, as Laidler Sunbeams and they were to grow up with lasting and grateful memories. Some of them still have reunions at the Victoria Hotel, Bradford, where Francis Laidler lived for some thirty years and where a bar with an adjacent dining-room was opened in August 1982, bearing his name.

There is always somebody who wants to make trouble, of course. Not only were there those who tried to make it more difficult, if not impossible, to obtain the necessary stage licences for the Sunbeams, but one local politician was nationally reported by the Press Association as claiming that conditions for children in the Bradford and Leeds pantomimes were worse than those under the half-time system.

Laidler was appalled. "I apply each year for pantomime licences for the Sunbeams," he said, "so this critic cannot claim, as an excuse for her terrible accusations that she was not fully conversant with the conditions regarding my Sunbeams.

"The Sunbeams appearing in my last season's pantomime at the Theatre Royal, Leeds, attended my Leeds school with regular punctuality; in fact with almost full attendance. The Sunbeams in my Bradford pantomime attended their own schools in Bradford.

"The inference ... is that the Sunbeams appeared at every matinee throughout last pantomime season. That is not so. During term time they appeared at only one matinee a week in addition to the Saturday matinee. The suggestions and allegations of over-work etc., are simply fantastic."

Those who had any experience of the Sunbeams set-up agreed. Fortunately, the truth was there for all to see when, on March 13th 1956, impresario Val Parnell, amid a distinguished company including Norman Evans, the pantomime dame, unveiled in the Alhambra foyer a memorial plaque, designed by Bradford's Mr. L. A. G. Heywood, R.I.B.A. It read: *A tribute to the King of Pantomime, Francis Laidler, A philanthropist who loved to make children happy."*

Unveiling the Laidler Plaque, 1956

From left to right: Norman Evans, Val Parnell, Mrs. G. S. Laidler, Alderman White and Bradford's Lady Mayoress, Mrs. Ruth.

By Courtesy of the Yorkshire Post

Far from exploiting any of the girls who flocked with their mothers to the Sunbeam auditions, Laidler considered their welfare of paramount importance. They had to be at least twelve years old, be in perfect health and to have evidence of regular school attendance during the six months preceding their acceptance. If they appeared in a panto which was not close to their homes, a large house was rented near the theatre, under the careful, caring eyes of a house-mother and her assistant.

As well as free accommodation and food, and a supply of pocket money, an amount was paid weekly into each girl's Post Office Savings Bank account. At the end of the panto's run each girl's bank book was handed to her parents. In addition, the Sunbeams were fitted out with an attractive uniform and if they passed you in the street they provided a sunny tribute to the avuncular character of Francis Laidler.

Enter Gwladys with a "W"

Among the seventy-five floral tributes at a funeral at Nab Wood Cemetery, Shipley, on Thursday, February 27th 1919, there was a particularly poignant one which read simply: "From the Little Sunbeams".

Annie Laidler had died five days earlier, on Saturday the 22nd, at the family home, 20 Marlborough Road, Manningham, Bradford, where, in ever-increasingly comfortable surroundings, she had lived with her husband and their four daughters, Marian, Ida, Bertha and Olive.

Her death had come while an influenza epidemic in Bradford was "assuming alarming proportions". During the week, no fewer than 313 deaths were reported in the city and of these 149 were attributed directly to influenza.

It had been only five years since Annie had officially opened her husband's new Alhambra. In spite of his loss, Laidler insisted on upholding the tradition of "the show must go on". He ordered that Monday's Variety performance must be presented as usual. Consequently, while he was grieving a reviewer was writing: "Mr. J. W. Rickaby, the well-known comedian, brought the house down with his efforts".

Not only did Laidler throw himself into the work of preparing more pantomimes, but he also stepped up his activities as a producer of applaud-winning touring revues. He also squeezed in time as a talent-spotter, and it was in this capacity he was to be found, six months after his wife's death, in the summer of 1919, at the Central Pier, Blackpool, where, under the management of Fred Allendale, the Premier Pierrots were the resident attraction.

One of the Pierrots caught his eye. He was immediately impressed by her vivacity, her engaging boyish style, her generous curvaceousness, her determined sparkle and her happy smile. Born Gladys Florence Cotterill, in Staffordshire, she was twenty-three — nineteen years younger than the man who was convinced he had found an artiste of distinction in the making.

His conviction was so strong that he wanted to know more about the girl who was obviously putting her heart and soul into her pom-poms-and-ruffles performance. He was surprised to discover that far from having a theatrical background, Gladys had been reared in the country where the professional theatre was still regarded by many as the haunt of the devil. Such a thing as a theatrical career for a young girl who had been carefully educated and sheltered from the world was not to be thought of.

In spite of this Gladys developed an urge to sing and act, finding a modest outlet for her talent during the 1914-18 war when she acquired a little concert party work at a military camp near her home. This subsequently led to an audition for the Premier Pierrots, who promptly engaged her.

Even though she had been on the professional stage for only two weeks, Francis Laidler was certain she was destined to be outstanding and didn't hesitate in inviting her to play second boy in *Aladdin,* his next pantomime at his Leeds Theatre Royal. Gladys gratefully accepted.

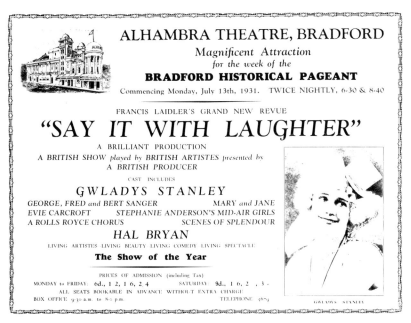

ALHAMBRA THEATRE, BRADFORD

Magnificent Attraction
for the week of the
BRADFORD HISTORICAL PAGEANT
Commencing Monday, July 13th, 1931.   TWICE NIGHTLY, 6·30 & 8·40

FRANCIS LAIDLER'S GRAND NEW REVUE

"SAY IT WITH LAUGHTER"

A BRILLIANT PRODUCTION
A BRITISH SHOW *played by* BRITISH ARTISTES *presented by*
A BRITISH PRODUCER

CAST INCLUDES

GWLADYS STANLEY

GEORGE, FRED *and* BERT SANGER   MARY *and* JANE
EVIE CARCROFT   STEPHANIE ANDERSON'S MID-AIR GIRLS
A ROLLS ROYCE CHORUS   SCENES OF SPLENDOUR

HAL BRYAN

LIVING ARTISTES LIVING BEAUTY LIVING COMEDY LIVING SPECTACLE

The Show of the Year

PRICES OF ADMISSION (including Tax)
MONDAY to FRIDAY: 6d., 1 2, 1 6, 2, 4   SATURDAY   9d., 1 6, 2 , 3 ·
ALL SEATS BOOKABLE IN ADVANCE WITHOUT EXTRA CHARGE
BOX OFFICE 9·30 a.m. to 8·0 p.m.   TELEPHONE 5679

GWLADYS STANLEY

Enter Gwladys with a "w"

During the panto's run Laidler said to her: "You will one day be a very good principal boy". Gladys later recalled: "Little did I think when I was saying my first few lines on the stage of the Leeds Royal that I would one day own that theatre".

The following year saw Gladys again playing second boy in *Aladdin,* this time in Bradford. Her song *I've lost my Cecilia* became all the rage and after hearing her sing this number Laidler said to her: "I want you to be my principal boy at the Prince's next year, but I don't wish you to tell anyone. Keep it a secret". And she did, even after signing a contract at Laidler's home where his secretary was also sworn to secrecy.

During the summer Laidler wrote to Gladys, telling her that she was to play Prince Charming in *Cinderella;* and by the end of the year the secret was out when her name appeared prominently on the bill-posters for the 1921-22 pantomime.

The name read Gwladys Stanley (the surname being that of her husband Albert Herbert Stanley, a man about whom we know little and from whom she obtained a divorce) and it soon became famous. The first name, Gwladys, which in its lettering had been given a theatrical flourish, was spelt in the manner which from then on had journalists always emphasising, when dictating to copytakers, "Don't forget! It's Gwladys with a 'w'".

The Fall into Love

During the run of the 1921-22 *Cinderella,* Gwladys Stanley fell on the Prince's stage and sprained an ankle. "That settled the matter," said Laidler. The pluck she showed very much deepened my admiration. She felt a great deal of pain but she carried on bravely with her song as though nothing had happened. When she came off-stage she collapsed in the wings, had to be taken home and was off for a few nights. I knew then that I was in love.''

When Gwladys returned to the Prince's, Laidler made up his mind then and there. He went straight to her dressing-room and said: ''Will you be my wife?'' The question was typical of Laidler's plucky directness — even if it took aback the woman who had developed considerable affection for this man who had given her her first big opportunity in the theatre.

''I think I said, 'Oh, dear!''' Gwladys once told me. ''I was touched and honoured and I happily accepted — after a long pause when you could have heard a pin drop. From that moment we were unofficially engaged. Francis, I remember, immediately invited my mother and father to meet him.''

The engagement was not announced until four years later. It was made known publicly in January 1926 when Gwladys was playing principal boy in *The Queen of Hearts* at the Palace Theatre, Manchester. By then Francis had prepared two homes — at 15 Park Mansions, Knightsbridge, London, and Room Nos. 25-26 on the first floor of the Great Northern Hotel, Bradford, the suite which was to be his almost constant residence in his later years.

The wedding took place at the Princes Row Register Office, Buckingham Palace Road, London, on April 22nd 1926. The couple thought they had kept the occasion a secret to all but the small and select company of people they had invited, but news of the impending marriage had leaked out in Fleet Street and a formidable battery of photographers lay in wait.

After the ceremony the new Mr. and Mrs. Laidler drove to the Hyde Park Hotel where the guests were entertained at a reception, during which a telegram from the civic head of Bradford (Alderman J. Stringer) was read out: ''*Hearty* congratulations and best wishes for your future happiness ... Lord Mayor of Bradford''.

Perhaps the most impressive feature of the reception was the wedding cake, which stood two-feet high. It was an exact miniature of the Alhambra Theatre.

Early in the afternoon the bride and groom left London for their honeymoon which was to be spent in Paris and Nice. They could be abroad for only ten days because they had to prepare for the launching of Laidler's three autumn revues. One of these was called *Glad Eyes* (''The nearest I could get to Gwladys'', said Laidler) and the others were entitled *Roundabout* and *Sun Rays*.

The Golden Age of Variety

The 1920's were heralded at the Alhambra by a spirit of zestful cameraderie. It was personified by a tiny, graceful and trim woman, of enormous vim, who stepped back on stage at the end of her act on November 29th 1919, to be presented with a two-handled, 13½ inch high silver Loving Cup bearing the inscription: ''To Vesta Tilley from Bradford admirers''.

The superb male impersonator, who hadn't an iota of masculinity in her, and who had the nation singing *Following in Father's Footsteps, Jolly Good Luck to the Girl who Loves a Soldier* and *The Army of Today's All Right,* wiped away a very feminine tear. At fifty-five she was making her farewell tour, but it wasn't having to say goodbye to her career which brought the moisture to her eyes. It was the joy of realising how much she had been appreciated in Bradford — where her husband, Sir Walter De Freece, was Francis Laidler's first partner in the booking of variety acts.

Bradford's variety-goers didn't simply like Vesta Tilley — they worshipped her. And she reciprocated. The same week she was given the Loving Cup she handed over the whole of her salary to the Bradford Cinderella Club for less fortunate children to endow a cot at the Hest Bank holiday home at Morecambe.

The sum was £500 — an enormous sum then, making many later pop stars' earnings look like pittances. The salary was evidence of the tremendous esteem in which she was held, an esteem highlighted when she handed the money to the club's president. Mr. H.C. Derwent, general manager of the Bradford and District Newspaper Co. Ltd. which, in 1926, was to become the 'parent' of the Telegraph & Argus.

If Vesta Tilley (a Gloucester music-hall manager's daughter who died in 1952 aged eighty-eight) was leaving the new decade at the Alhambra to others, they were not all going to say a big thank-you.

One who certainly wasn't going to be pleased was George Robey (who was knighted towards the end of his life and who died two years after Vesta Tilley at the age of eighty-five).

George Robey — "The Prime Minister of Mirth" — was one of the stand-up comics who gave Variety its backbone character. This, however, didn't impress some of the audiences of Bradford where George appeared more than once at the Alhambra (brave man!). Quite simply, some of his patter was not to their liking.

George knew it — and got his own back. In a seventieth birthday interview he explained: "London audiences are good. They are out to enjoy themselves. Some provincial audiences are very good and some very bad. Bradford, for example, is known as the deathbed of comedians. If they don't like a man, the whole of the front row of the stalls can take up their evening papers and read.

"Once when I went to Bradford I sang them three songs and I did them three patters, and I don't think I got a smile. So when I came back to take a call I thought I'd invent a little story for them.

"I told them that I'd left London the night before to come up to play for them: that I'd waited in a queue at King's Cross ticket office, and as I got up to the booking clerk I said: 'I want to go to Bradford', and the booking clerk said to me: 'You don't mean you *want* to go to Bradford; you mean you've got to'. Well, they listened to me after that!"

Fortunately there were performers who *did* want to go to Bradford once the Alhambra had made its mark — hundreds of them! Throughout the thriving years of Variety there was hardly a star or a star-in-the-making who did not appear on its stage.

It would be impossible to write about them all, but there are a number of artists who have made an important contribution to the Alhambra's history and whose names evoke a flavour of the past, like those *Veterans of Variety* in 1923, who included Tom Costello, Len Dryeden, Arthur Roberts and Charles Bignell. More evocative to most people today are the names Nervo and Knox who shared the same bill. As "representatives of the new school", they were thought to be very daring funnymen even if their material would have seemed tame during the later years of the famous Crazy Gang they were to join.

George Formby Snr. made his last appearance at the Alhambra in August 1920. He had for long jested on stage about his wheeze and his "coughing better", but most of his audience didn't realise that the affliction was real and he had suffered for years from a chest complaint from which he died the following year.

In August 1921 a lanky lad made his entrance on the Alhambra boards under the name of George Hoy, a name in very small print on the bill-posters. He was Formby's son and he was using his father's material because he had no other! He was only seventeen and had never, prior to this tour, been on a stage.

He was far from being a success, alas, but with the help and encouragement of a performer who had been in the same show he managed to find some new comedy material. He also found eventually that ukelele which, together with his cheeky Lancashire accent, was to make the "new" George Formby, one of the true greats of Variety, and a regular Alhambra idol.

During this period considerable promise was shown by an effervescent beauty called Florence Desmond. She made her first appearance at the Alhambra in a 1927 revue called *Piccadilly* in which Max Miller also appeared. Six years earlier this "Cheeky Chappie" had found early experience at the Lidget Green Pavilion, Bradford.

A former C. B. Cochran chorus girl (like Anna Neagle who was revered by Alhambra audiences), Florence was so multi-gifted that she was almost *too* talented. No one knew which performer's tag to give her. Noel Coward observed that "Flo is a jack-of-all-trades and a master of none". He strongly advised her to specialise. She took his advice and became one of the best stage impressionists ever. The influence of her artistry still survives.

If you sought further elegant humour at the Alhambra in the old days, it was offered in abundance by George Lashwood and Randolph Sutton, two Titans of their time.

Lashwood dressed so elegantly that he was known as "The Beau Brummel of the Halls" and no-one could dispute the fact that he had a wardrobe which would have made many a Regency buck envious. During his prime, commercial song-plugging was still in the future and most popular songs were associated with the Variety performers who first sang them. Consequently *The Man Who Broke the Bank at Monte Carlo* was (and still is) associated with Charles Coburn, while *Champagne Charlie* was popularised by George Leybourne.

Lashwood was acknowledged to be Leybourne's successor and just as good. *In the Twi-Twi-Twilight* was one of his big hits, whilst other songs of his they raved about were *Where Are the Lads of the Village, The Gallant Twenty-First* and *Three Women to Every Man.* One of the highest paid light comedians ever, Lashwood was married to Edith Finck who appeared in many of George Edwardes' musical comedies and who was principal girl in the *Puss in Boots* pantomime at the Bradford Theatre Royal in 1902-03, when Francis Laidler was just starting at the Prince's.

Tall and immaculate, Bristol-born Randolph Sutton was a master of feather-light humour and the supremo of the songs he made famous. *On Mother Kelly's Doorstep* and *Bye, Bye, Blackbird* were two of them. As a youth he was recommended by comedian Leslie Henson to a West End management and was offered a three-year contract. He turned it down. "I wouldn't go", he told me, "because I knew I still wasn't fit to do so". How many pop and rock aspirants today could match the wisdom of that self-knowledge?

On the same bill when George Lashwood made his last appearance at the Alhambra was "Your own, your very own, Jack Pleasants". This Bradford comedian, whose speciality was his shy delivery, was much loved in the Halls, with his sombre billycock hat off-set by the huge daisy in his lapel. (Ken Dodd, with a similar bloom, was to carry on his crazy flower-power.)

Jack, who was born in 1875, began his career in the singing rooms of Bradford and Leeds, including the Old Crown, Ivegate, in his native city. His hit songs included *I'm Shy Mary Ellen, I'm Shy* and of course the one which nearly everyone has sung, *I'm Twenty-One Today*. If you want an idea of how shy Jack performed it, sing it simperingly and much, much slower than you hear it at parties. The likelihood is that you will then say to yourself, "How is such a soppy birthday boy going to survive?". But then, that was the reaction Jack Pleasants sought.

Sadly, Jack collapsed on the stage of the Bradford Prince's Theatre on Boxing Day, 1923, while playing Simple Simon in a Francis Laidler pantomime. Appendicitis was a major surgery case in those days and Jack never returned to the stage. He died the following year.

Although Variety was paramount in the Alhambra's early years, this didn't keep other forms of entertainment off its stage. Musical comedy was an early favourite and so were its stars, including one of the greatest of all time. Born in 1879 in a back-to-back house in Drewton Street, Bradford — hardly a stone's throw from the Theatre Royal in Manningham Lane — she was Gertie Millar, for years the toast of London's Gaiety and Daly's theatres, and the darling of the West End.

Bradford's own Gertie Millar as The Quaker Girl

Gertie was not a stunning beauty like, say, Gabrielle Ray, who starred at the Alhambra too. But she did have bewitching eyes, a sweetly turned-up nose, a graceful figure and a piquant magic which, in musical comedies like *Our Miss Gibbs* and *Gipsy Love,* had the capital at her pretty feet. They just couldn't credit that she was "a lass fra' Brattfud".

In 1900 a thirty year-old bachelor booked a seat at the Theatre Royal, Bradford to see the twenty-one year-old local girl who was lighting up the stage with her charm. She was to sing a song he composed for *The Messenger Girl* in which she was appearing. He had heard that her fame was spreading quickly in Yorkshire and Lancashire.

His name was Lionel Monckton, the son of the Town Clerk of the City of London. Monckton, whose magic illuminated such shows as *The Arcadians* and *The Quaker Girl* (Gertie was to create its title role), was not only impressed. He fell in love with her. He persuaded his boss at the Gaiety Theatre, the renowned George Edwardes, to see her and he promptly cast her in *The Toreador*. The rest is theatre history. She became a superstar almost over-night and Monckton married her. After his death a quarter of a century later, she married the Earl of Dudley to become the Countess of Dudley. She died in April 1952.

Gertie Millar had her first schooling at Christ Church Schools not far from her home in Drewton Street, a thoroughfare then much associated with theatrical lodgings. She made her stage debut as a bashful little girl on a concert platform at Pudsey and from this came regular engagements on Saturday evenings at the Mechanics' Institute, Bradford.

One evening Arthur Brogden, founder of the Swiss Choir which toured the country and happened to have a booking in Bradford, saw her. She was then about twelve. He engaged her as a juvenile member of the choir and she toured with it until she was seventeen when she came back to her home town, as an established juvenile star, to take an important part in a Bradford pantomime. Her success in this led to her appearing in numerous big shows in the north, including *The Messenger Girl,* in which Monckton originally saw her.

A myth still lingers that Gertie once worked in a Bradford mill, but in a not widely published interview in the early 1930's, Gertie herself dismissed the idea. "It would not have bothered my head even if I had worked in a mill'', she said, adding: "I'm afraid I never did anything half so useful. If I had worked in a mill I should have been proud of the fact.'' The myth probably got round because of the leading part she played in a West End musical for which she was dressed as a clogs-and-shawl mill girl.

In the 1920's, Gertie (by then a countess) was persuaded by Francis Laidler to make a short "come-back" at the Alhambra, having officially retired in 1918. But memories of her remained strong with the people of her home town where, during a supposedly final appearance at the Alhambra, she had generously paid for a two-weeks' holiday for twenty children.

Gertie, who in 1930 was to give £1,000 to endow a bed at the new Bradford Infirmary in Duckworth Lane, thought that her 'mill' image from the London musical would go down well at her Alhambra "comeback". But Laidler advised her: "They won't want to see you in clogs and a shawl. They will want you to look beautiful in a lovely gown and jewels''.

They eventually agreed on a compromise — a first song in clogs and shawl and another in a glamourous gown and jewels. For the first number there was affectionate applause, but for the second there was an ovation.

"You were right", said Gertie. "They want to see me in diamonds''. Francis Laidler's theatrical instinct was, as usual, right.

Gaunt Days

During her Gaiety days, Gertie Millar had a dresser named Polly. She must have been extremely deft at handling the heavy, lavish stage costumes of the day, because lovely Gabrielle Ray employed her for a while in this capacity too. So did another queen of musical comedy who had Alhambra audiences ecstatic and who perhaps came closest to taking the crown from Gertie.

She was Jose Collins who, for an astonishing 1,352 performances non-stop at Daly's Theatre, London made *The Maid of the Mountains* hers for ever — even if during one period no less than fourteen travelling companies were presenting this tuneful romance throughout Britian. The original Daly's production opened in 1916 when Jose was twenty-eight.

She was the daughter of music-hall star Lottie Collins, who took London and then the whole country by storm with her *Ta-Ra-Ra-Boom-De-Ay* dancing. Both mother and daughter appeared in pantomime at the Bradford Theatre Royal during their early days — Lottie in 1884 and Jose in 1909-10. Directly after her pantomime appearance Jose went to America where, in 1911, she played the lead in *Vera Violetta* at the Winter Gardens, New York, and appeared in the *Ziegfeld Follies of 1913*. She then returned to London.

Jose Collins was one of the highest paid performers of her generation, yet, when she died, aged seventy-one in 1959, she didn't leave a penny. Her doctor husband lamented: "There was no estate, no probate, no will, absolutely nothing As fast as Jose earned money she spent it or gave it away.''

Most of those around Jose adored her, including dresser Polly, who accompanied her to Bradford in 1927 when she starred in *The Greek Slave*. Jose often sent Polly out to the nearest fish-and-chip shop for a fish-and-chips supper. It was one of her favourite dishes and, with much delight, she would recall sharing fish and chips from a newspaper with young Charlie Chaplin when he was appearing in Fred Karno's *Mumming Birds*.

It is ironic that Jose Collins, who died broke, should, during her richest London years, publicly express sympathy for the financial plight of the most exceptional Bradford wool merchant of this century — as well as a man who gave the Alhambra a week to remember.

He was William Clifford Gaunt who, in addition to running a colossal industrial empire, was dubbed "The Napoleon of the Stage". Billy, as he was called by all his friends, was so fascinated by the stage that he bought some of London's most famous theatres. His interest in this began on the day he met Sir George Dance, the celebrated librettist and theatre manager. He gave Sir George a cheque for £25,000 (a fantastic sum then) as a deposit for the purchase of the Gaiety, the Adelphi and the Shaftesbury theatres. Then he bought the Apollo and later gained control of the Winter Garden and His Majesty's Theatres.

It was Billy's money which gave her first leading role to Evelyn Laye, who years later was to star with Anton Walbrook at the Alhambra in the pre-West End premiere of the musical, *Wedding in Paris*. Jack Hulbert and Leslie Henson also rose to stardom in Billy's theatres. Because he loved his Yorkshire dialect, Billy would often converse in this manner with an equally eager buddy, the celebrated actor Henry Ainley.

In later life Billy reflected: "I backed scores of shows and at one time I had about £500,000 invested in London theatres. I once had a big interest in a major film producing company. I started a marine insurance company. I ran three farms and made them pay. I introduced the Packard car to this country. I once bought a ship. And I even ran rum and whisky to the United States during Prohibition. But the important thing, I suppose, is that I built up in thirty years the greatest one-man wool business the world has ever known."

Billy, one of whose sons was once engaged to Adele Astaire, sister of Fred Astaire, was one of the victims of a slump between the wars; and, before he died, aged sixty-nine, at his home at Apperley Bridge, Bradford, in December 1942, he could be found looking after a petrol station.

Jose Collins, at the time of the slump, said "Billy Gaunt was a millionaire several times over when he played the part of 'angel' to our Gaiety productions, and he really was an angel. Always courteous and diffident, he had a twinkle in his eye that was most disarming.

"When things were going well he just stood about and said everything was 'lovely', and if things were not so good he added that they would be 'lovely' again. He never grumbled and never interferred, and it was, I suppose, just as fascinating for him to get the same kind of kick out of owning theatres as he did out of owning race-horses.

"Certainly he had no ulterior motive, and I like to think that, although the slump had treated him badly, he came to no great harm as a result of his association with us. In spite of his great wealth he was an immense worker, and he would be in his city office long before most of us were thinking of getting out of bed."

Thanks to Billy Gaunt, two of the greatest names in the history of American musicals (though not at the time as famous as they were to become) visited the Alhambra in 1926 to supervise the production of their new show, *Lido Lady*. They were Richard Rodgers and Lorenz Hart, creators of such classics as *The Girl Friend, The Boys From Syracuse* and *Pal Joey*.

Lido Lady was written for Jack Hulbert and his wife Cicely Courtneidge and was not intended for the American market. It was presented by arrangement with Billy Gaunt and had its world premiere at the Alhambra on Monday, October 4th, before transferring to the Gaiety Theatre, London.

The *Bradford Daily Telegraph* critic began: "What might be described as a new style musical entertainment was on view at the Bradford Alhambra last night when *Lido Lady* made its first appearance on any stage.

"There is no doubt that *Lido Lady* scored one of the greatest successes ever known in Bradford. The house was filled to utmost capacity and the applause was prolonged and frequent."

After praising sky-high the company, especially Phyllis Dare, he went on: "Costumes and scenery have never been surpassed on any Bradford stage, or even equalled. It was one of the greatest first nights in the history of the Bradford theatre."

The Actor Managers

In the 1920's, and continuing into the 30's, Variety at the Alhambra was leavened not only by straight drama itself but by performances from some of the most outstanding actor-managers of the day, including Sir John Martin-Harvey and Matheson Lang.

Sir John, son of an Essex naval architect, was a genius of romantic costume drama, and tens of thousands thrilled to his portrayals in such favourites as *The King's Messenger, The Burgomaster of Stilemonds, The Corsican Brothers* and *The Only Way* — not to mention Shakespeare's *Henry V* and *Hamlet*.

After making his first appearance at the Old Court Theatre, London, under John Clayton, it was apparent that Martin-Harvey would have a successful stage career and he was engaged for one of Sir Charles Wyndham's noted companies. He later joined Sir Henry Irving, with whom he remained for several years, accompanying him on his various tours of America. Sir John was at various times manager of the Lyceum, London (home of some of Irving's greatest triumphs), and the Prince of Wales, Court, Royalty and Apollo theatres, London.

Like Matheson Lang, he was not ashamed of "hogging" the limelight and the masses, as well as the West End, adored him for it. Bradford was no exception; and in turn Martin-Harvey had much regard for the city. He described it in a letter as "that dear, smokey old city" and went on to write of his "unforgettable remembrance that it was at the Midland Hotel, Bradford, after his last performance of *Becket* at the Bradford Theatre Royal in October, 1905, that our beloved chief died". (He was referring, of course, to Irving.)

Sir John continued: "He was very exhausted, as you know, and I dare say you remember too that terribly heavy door in the Midland Hotel which you had to put all your weight against before you could swing it open. I sometimes wonder whether the last effort of his to open that door hastened the end."

Until the 1960's the Alhambra itself had a personal connection with that fateful evening at the Theatre Royal, for Fred Unwin, its nightwatchman and former stage-door keeper, had been call-boy at the Royal on the night of Irving's death.

"Sir Henry Irving was a very kind man," he told me. "If he hadn't been I might have been fired. It happened one night when Irving was preparing a costume drama. One of his assistants was wearing chain mail which clattered as he walked across the stage. I couldn't help shouting out in a stage whisper: 'You'd better get a pair of rubber heels'. The man started laughing, and if Irving hadn't seen the funny side, well ...".

Matheson Lang was a cousin of Archbishop Lang and was said to "own the handsomest legs on the stage, command the longest queues, and have a dignity that belongs to a courtlier generation than his own."

He always remained tremendously fit, thanks partly to the athletic encouragement he received from his old boss, Sir Frank Benson, another Alhambra star. As a young man, Lang was a member of Sir Frank's Shakespearean company, but received his first big break when he was cast in a leading part in an American tour with Mrs. Langtry, the 'Jersey Lily', a tour which was loosely a subject of the Judge Bean film starring Paul Newman.

Returning to Britain, Lang became the youngest *Hamlet* in London long before he achieved fame in his greatest successes — *Mr. Wu, The Chinese Bungalow, Blood and Sand, Jew Suss* and, perhaps most admired of all, *The Wandering Jew*. He visited

Bradford on numerous occasions, the first being in *Under Cover* at the Empire in 1917, and the last, in 1935 at the Alhambra in *For the Defence*.

Stage performers are notoriously superstitious and are among the keenest collectors of talismans, but the one which Matheson Lang brought to the Alhambra was unusual to say the least. It was a small cedar wood box which somebody offered to buy from him for a small fortune, but which women wouldn't even dare touch. Lang called it his "Wandering Jew" box because it had been presented to him by a woman who had been so impressed by his performance in this drama about a man condemned to roam the world for eternity that she had seen the play eighty times.

She told Lang how, a hundred years previously, one of her ancestors on a visit to Tunis had assisted a Jew who was ill in the street and had taken him home. The Jew was in rags but his house was beautifully furnished and full of precious antiques. When the "good Samaritan" expressed surprise and asked the Jew who, or what, he was, he received the reply: "You may laugh at me and you may even think me mad, but I am the Wandering Jew".

For this kindness the visitor was given the small cedar wood box. It was obviously very old and it contained three moonstones and an uncut diamond. He was told that it would bring him and other men who eventually possessed it good fortune, but that it would bring bad luck to any woman who owned it. The box was eventually given to the woman who presented it to Matheson Lang. Her husband and two sons were killed in the 1914-18 war and, remembering the history of the box, she dcided to give it away.

Matheson Lang later insisted that he was no more superstitious than the average person, although he observed the traditional theatrical "rules" of not whistling in someone's dressing-room, never leaving a cake of soap behind or quoting the "Scottish play" and never saying the last line of a play at rehearsal. Nevertheless, he said he would hate to lose the box. "From the moment that lady handed it to me," he said, "I have had wonderfully good luck. My dresser puts it out for me every night and I wouldn't be without it for the world."

A Full House in 1932

32

Panto Time

Francis Laidler presented his first pantomime at the Prince's Theatre for the season of 1902-03 and in conjunction with his partner, Walter Piper. During 1903, however, Piper died suddenly and Laidler was faced with the prospect of mounting the next season's pantomime, *Aladdin,* on his own.

As his first solo venture into pantomime it was vital that *Aladdin* should be a success and to produce it he brought in a man whose name is still known to many because of the Variety circuit which bore his name. He was Frank MacNaghten, who was assisted at the Prince's by stage manager Harry Drury, and who numbered among the theatres of which he was proprietor The Palace, Bradford; The Palace, Halifax; The Grand Theatre, Sheffield; The Palace, Blackburn; The Tivoli, Leicester; the King's Theatre, Nottingham; The Palace, Lincoln and, prize of them all, Sadler's Wells Theatre, London. He was also managing director of theatres at Rotherham, Chesterfield, Attercliffe and Bow, London.

Aladdin was specially written for the Prince's by J. H. Wolfe, with local and topical allusions by Arthur W. Field. The music was arranged and conducted by Carl Hamblin, with special numbers by Fred Trussell of the London Hippodrome. Messrs. Hinton and Co. of London designed and painted the "magnificent scenery", while the mechanical effects were by A. Montague of Westminster. The pantomime starred the sisters Violet, Minnie and Marie Silcott, Ruby Winstone, Bob Selvidge, May Maple, George Collins, Gilbert Rodgers, Fred Maple, Sandy and Carl, and Mr. F. Martino.

Aladdin turned out to be a huge success and during its production Laidler learned so much from Frank MacNaghten that by the following season he felt sufficiently confident to take over the producer's chair himself. He held it firmly from then on.

For all his activities as an impresario and his pleasure in presenting first-class Variety and big touring shows, panto remained his passion and by 1930-31, when he transferred his pantomimes to the Alhambra, he had few equals in that field.

If he had any secrets of success, there were two. The first was his ability to put himself completely into the creation of his pantos — so completely that to him all those principal boys and girls, princes and princesses, droll dames and fearsome giants, fairy queens and jolly village-green dancers, were even more real to him than they were to the children in his audiences.

The second was his seeminlgy infinite capacity for hard work. This did not go unnoticed by celebrated theatre artist Stanley Parker when he came to sketch Francis Laidler. He thought the "upward trend" of Laidler's "moustachios and astonishing eyebrows" gave him the appearance of a demon king — "a demon for work!"

Laidler started work immediately after an 8 a.m. breakfast and, during pantomime runs, rarely finished before bedtime — and that was never before 11 p.m. When his pantomimes were running simultaneously at Bradford, Leeds, London, Newcastle, Sheffield, Manchester, Nottingham and Bristol, he often found it necessary to do a day's work and then travel through the night to a place 200 miles away to be ready to start another day's work.

But for all the pressures on him, he was never one of those wildly gesticulating, abrasive producers who so easily get into a panic. If he did wish to admonish someone an icy look from those astute grey eyes was sufficient — the same eyes which would light up whenever he planned his pantos with the help of his beloved miniature theatre whose tiny stage meant the world to him, the world of his fairy-tale imagination.

Laidler, whose favourite pantomime was *Mother Goose,* with *Cinderella* a close second, rarely spoke publicly about his panto work. He was a "do-er, not a talker". But occasionally, when he did speak about it, his love for it shone through. When TV first boomed, for instance, he was asked about the effect it was having on the stage, many theatres having found business diving.

"In my particular case," he answered, "I counter the competition with better pantomime. In the coming pantomime season I will face the challenge of TV, or any other factor, by presenting an entirely new production. Would I risk many thousands of pounds on an entirely new production if I had not confidence in its success? Over the years there have been several crises, like industrial depressions, the cinema, talking pictures and radio. I faced up to them, and I'm facing up to TV."

The tremendous faith Francis Laidler had in his pantomimes was never misdirected and the place they won in the family life of Bradford and Leeds became almost as dear to the public as Christmas itself. He left a great panto legacy and it was as well he did, for without pantomimes the Alhambra would never have survived the bleak years before the "resurrection" made possible by the 1986 improvements.

There were a few who didn't agree with him, nevertheless. One of them was Maurice Webb, a Bradford M.P. and one-time Minister of Agriculture. He complained that the lovers of other kinds of stage entertainment were for too many weeks denied their preference because of long-running pantomimes at the Alhambra.

Of medium stature he might have been, but Francis Laidler fought back like a lion when he informed Mr. Webb, if in more gentlemanly words, that he was talking rubbish. "As I have pointed out on previous occasions," he said, "during the Christmas season almost all variety stars and good variety acts are booked to appear in resident pantomimes up and down the country and therefore they are unable to tour in variety shows in the provinces. It would be found to be practically impossible to book a succession of really good variety bills during the general pantomime season, should it be desired to do so.

"During the year at the Alhambra every endeavour is made to book the very best possible entertainment for all types of Bradford theatregoer; such as the great variety stars, the premier grand opera and ballet companies and star attractions such as the recent *Gay Rosalina, King's Rhapsody, Annie Get Your Gun* and *Oklahoma!* I am anxious to adopt the policy of satisfying the widest possible demand."

As usual, Laidler knew what he was talking about, a characteristic of this man with a pawky humour of his own and one which was in evidence again during the matter of the Demon King.

In London an authority on stage artistry was widely reported when, during a lecture sponsored by the British Drama League, he insisted that the Demon Kings of pantomime were "no longer appearing as if by magic through the stage floor" because the trap work was too dangerous. "It is extremely perilous work," he was quoted as saying, "for if the actor stood a little to one side, or not quite upright on the platform, he could easily hit the edge of the stage floor and kill himself. There are now very few people who do trap work. Trap work like all clowning, runs in families and these have now died out."

Laidler was much amused when told of this. "I go entirely against the speaker," he said. "I can get trap artists just when I want. They are not 'Demon Kings' who rise up, but the 'Slaves of the Lamp' in the *Aladdin* pantomines. There is no danger at all if one is acquainted with the working.

"The speaker is exaggerating the danger. I myself have come up the star trap on the last night of the pantomime, but, of course, not at the speed of the professional 'slave'. I have also gone on the flying ballet, as Bradford's theatregoers know, but not very fast or high. I can employ artists for the star trap effect any time I want them." And he could.

During his career Francis Laidler produced over 250 pantomines, more than any other producer before or since — an even more momentous achievement when you remember that he was thirty-six when he presented his first. Of that number, twenty-two were staged at the Alhambra — every one of which was a winner because he took such a close personal interest in them.

Sometimes he would be in the prompt box night after night, supervising and keeping an eye out for any "Stage-door Johnnies" trying to sneak in. He was adamant about this and would allow no-one backstage, not even the Press, unless he himself accompanied them.

Yet he was still a kindly and considerate man. The welfare of his artists was especially important to him, particularly the welfare of his little Sunbeams, every one of whom he knew by name. "They were treated as if they were my own children," he would say. Each year at the Victoria Hotel he would give a big tea-party for the Sunbeams, as well as encouraging them to present a special private performance of the pantomime they were in. This time *they* played all the grown-up parts and the watching adult principals loved it.

However, even with his intense interest in his beloved Alhambra, Laidler still had to be here, there and everywhere to ensure that his other pantos were running smoothly.

At the same time as his 1938-39 *Aladdin* pantomime was running at the Alhambra, for example, he produced *Red Riding Hood* at the Royal Opera House, Covent Garden. Starring Patricia Burke (as Prince Charming), Nelson Keys (Mother Hubbard), George Jackley (Simple Simon), Polly Ward (Red Riding Hood) and Arthur Rees (King Wolf), it was one of several triumphant London pantomimes which Laidler produced in the 1930's and early 40's.

Red Riding Hood was seen by Her Majesty Queen Elizabeth and her daughters, Princess Elizabeth and Princess Margaret Rose. Many years later, when the then Queen Mother attended the first Bradford Delius Festival, she said how delighted the three of them had been by that panto and how cherished was the memory.

After the success of *Red Riding Hood* Laidler said: "Covent Garden used to have pantomimes every Christmas and I wanted to revive the old traditions. My maxims are the same for London as for the provinces. I believe in sticking to the half-dozen subjects which have a good plot. I carry the story through and never degrade it with extraneous Variety turns which have nothing to do with the theme.

"I used all the apparatus of the stage for my spectacular effects, the cyclorama, the traps and the raises. I had a flying ballet and made Red Riding Hood float across the stage on unseen wires. And I had a Harlequinade, following the tradition of the Opera House where John Rich developed the art and was himself the greatest of Harlequins."

He went on: "The humour was natural to the story and wholesome. I do not allow any suggestive jokes. Happily I had the London audience singing. Pantomime is a sociable entertainment and people like to join in the choruses."

Laidler then insisted: "The old fairy stories as I tell them will never lose their appeal for children, both young and old. I am convinced that pantomime will still be going strong at the end of another fifty years."

Laidler's first West End pantomime was presented at Daly's Theatre, for a long time the home of *The Merry Widow*. The panto was *Mother Goose* and the year was 1932. It is believed to be the only pantomime ever staged there and it starred Cora Goffin and George Lacey.

Among his other West End shows were his 1934-35 *Babes in the Wood* at the Victoria Palace, starring his wife Gwladys Stanley, Mary Daly and Duggie Wakefield, and several pantos at the London Coliseum where, in 1942-43, there appeared in *Mother Goose* one of the great successes of his Alhambra pantos, Norman Evans.

Francis Laidler Pantomimes and the Alhambra Pantos which followed them

- 1902-3, *Red Riding Hood:* Gracie Graham, Fanny Harris, Percy Curry, Guy Drury, Teddy Gibbs.
- 1903-4, *Aladdin:* Violet and Marie Silcott, Bob Selvidge, T. B. Fayme.
- 1904-5, *Robinson Crusoe:* Adela Rose, Lily Black, Billy Elliott, Oliver Conroy.
- 1905-6, *Dick Whittington:* Esme Gordon, Edith Ager, Percy Curry, T. B. Fayme.
- 1906-7, *Cinderella:* Florrie Forde, Alice Williams, Nellie Sheffield, Jo Monkhouse.
- 1907-8, *Aladdin:* Lillie Soutter, Ethel Bryant, Bert Byrne, Frank Robinson, Dan Hardie.
- 1908-9, *Red Riding Hood:* Florrie Forde, Susie Belmore, Victoria Cross, Bert Bryne, Will Lindsay, Frank Robinson.
- 1909-10, *Forty Thieves:* Ada Fawn, Lesley Gibson, May Mannering, Dick Tubb, Alf Corrie, Chris le Brun, Frank Robinson.
- 1910-11, *Babes In The Wood:* Florrie Forde, Susie Belmore, Bob Selvidge, George Brooks, Willie Leopold, Victor Crawford, Gilbert Rogers.
- 1911-12, *Dick Whittington:* Barbara Babbington, Mona Vivian, Olive Pursell, Bert Byrne, Tom Bates, Hector Gordon.
- 1912-13, *Cinderella:* Alice Wyatt, Susie Belmore, Gypsie Hodgson, Minnie Myrie, Reg Bolton, Victor Crawford, Fred Anderson.
- 1913-14, *Robinson Crusoe:* Alice Wyatt, Molly McCarthy, Mamie Watson, Lucy Murray, Bob Selvidge, Syd Howard, Leslie Barker, Fred Anderson.
- 1914-15, *Aladdin:* Mona Vivian, Aimee Stewart, Minnie Myrle, Reg Bolton, Will Lindsay, Norman H. Lee.
- 1915-16, *Cinderella:* Rene Ralph, Empsie Bowman, Walter Amner, Brothers Obo, Percy Cahill, Milton Brothers.
- 1916-17, *Dick Whittington:* Mona Vivian, Daisy West-Collins, Bob Selvidge, Brothers Obo.
- 1917-18, *Robin Hood:* Lily Vine, Winnie Goodwin, Fred Walmsley, May Sherrard, Adrian Ross.

- 1918-19, *Forty Thieves:* Winifred Ward, Lottie Govell, Brothers Obo, Ken Kendrick, Bob Selvidge, Frank Lilliput.
- 1919-20, *Babes In The Wood:* Gabrielle Ray, Nellie Gallafent, Gwennie Harcourt, Fred Walmsley, Leslie Barker.
- 1920-21, *Aladdin:* Gwladys Stanley, Bobbie Macaulay, Aimee Stewart, G. S. Melvin, Brothers Obo, Pat Redmond, Harry Thornton.
- 1921-22, *Cinderella:* Gwladys Stanley, Cecilia Gold, Chick Farr, Leslie Barker, Jimmy Pullin, Pat Redmond.
- 1922-23, *Dick Whittington:* Rene Ralph, Dot Temple, Cissie Sullivan, Tom D. Newell, Tom Drew, Tom Morton, Walter Waite.
- 1923-24, *Red Riding Hood:* Dorothy Leigh, Winifred O'Connor, Jack Pleasants, John E. Coyle, Hobbs and Nolan, Gwennie Harcourt.
- 1924-25, *Robinson Crusoe:* Cissie Sullivan, Dorothy Viggers, Marion Dawson, Naughton and Gold, Nor Kiddie.
- 1925-26, *Babes In The Wood:* Daisy Taylor, Irene North, Reg Bolton, Tom Prior, Eddie Foy.
- 1926-27, *Dick Whittington:* Margery Wyn, Jane Ayr, Harry Angers, Jack and George McNaughton, Stuart Watson.
- 1927-28, *Cinderella:* Ouida Macdermott, Betty Green, Marion Dawson, Madge White, Tom Prior.
- 1928-29, *Aladdin:* Vera Vere, Jessie Moore, Frederic Culpitt, Queen and Le Brun, Hal Bert, St. John Sisters.
- 1929-30, *Jack and the Beanstalk:* Madge White, Betty Davies, Mark Daly.
- 1930-31, *Mother Goose:* Norah Blaney, George Lacy, Joan Brett, Marie Picquart.
- 1931-32, *Humpty Dumpty:* Nita Underwood, Gwen May, Dolores and Cecelia Nono, Bertram Dench, Hugh Rene, Ivor Vintor.
- 1932-33, *Babes In the Wood:* Irene Lister, Noreen Davies, Mary O'Hara, Norman Griffin, Albert Modley.

- 1933-34, *Dick Whittington:* Eileen Midgley, Evie Carcraft, Albert Modley, Dick Evans.
- 1934-35, *Red Riding Hood:* Phyllis Godden, Bessie Pratt, Jennie Gregson, Fred Walmsley, Roy Barbour.
- 1935-36, *Cinderella:* Phyllis Godden, Bessie Pratt, Ivy Luck, Marion Dawson, Reg Bolton, Claude Worth.
- 1936-37, *Mother Goose:* Rosalind Melville, Iris Sadler, Marion Gerth, Doreen Cheyne, Joan Preston, Albert Modley.
- 1937-38, *Babes In The Wood:* Robin Coles, Elsie Tree, Fred Walmsley, Holt and Maurice, Betty Conquest.
- 1938-39, *Aladdin:* Frank Randle, Peggy Bedall, Iris Sadler.
- 1939-40, *Mother Goose:* Margaret Morgan, Pauline Lewis, Marion Dawson, Albert Modley, Darroll Richards.
- 1940-41, *Jack and the Beanstalk:* June Bardsley, Joy Francis, Norman Evans, George Baines, Percy Garside, Hal Osmond.
- 1941-42. *Red Riding Hood:* Veronica Duke, Anne Singer, Marie Delaislane, Phil Strickland, Jack Hayes, Percy Garside.
- 1942-43, *Cinderella:* Rosalind Melville, Pauline Lewis, Georgette Perry, Muriel White, Bunny Doyle, Rich and Galvin, Wilfred Watson, Billy Purvis.
- 1943-44, *Humpty Dumpty:* Grace Draper, Irlin Hall, Norman Evans, Betty Jumel, Percy Garside, Charlie Jass.
- 1944-45, *Aladdin:* Sylvia Kellaway, Audrey Hewitt, Bunny Doyle, Bert Rich, Wilfred Watson, Billy Purvis.
- 1945-46, *Jack and the Beanstalk:* Bunty Meadows, Gloria Starr, Sonia Stacpoole, Roy Barbour, Jack Hayes.
- 1946-47, *Mother Goose:* Norman Evans, Margery Manners, Betty Martin, Betty Jumel, Percy Garside, Edgar Driver, Richard Milner, Billy Purvis.
- 1947-48, *Cinderella:* Wilfred Pickles, June Whitfield, Fay Lenore, Marion Dawson, Bert Rich, Richard Milner.

- 1948-49, *Red Riding Hood:* Norman Evans, Margery Manners, Mary Merodith, Percy Garside, Billy Purvis.
- 1949-50, *Humpty Dumpty:* Albert Modley, Margery Manners, Bonnie Downs, Deirdrie Peyer.
- 1950-51, *Aladdin:* Zena Dell, Mary Allen, Claude Chandler, Rob Currie, Alex Lennox, Percy Garside, Billy Purvis.
- 1951-52, *Cinderella:* Kathleen West, Walter Niblo, Joy Beattie, Jasmine Dee, Trevor Morton.
- 1952-53, *Mother Goose:* Jack Storey, Doreen Duke, Bonnie Downs, Hackford and Doyle.
- 1953-54, *Jack and the Beanstalk:* Bunny Doyle, Betty Dayne, The Romas.
- 1954-55, *Red Riding Hood,* Jack Storey, Jasmine Dee, Viki Emra.
- 1955-56, *Robin Hood:* Jimmy Paige, Eddie Henderson, Call McCord and his horse Ladybird.
- 1956-57, *The Sleeping Beauty:* Billy Whitaker, Joe Black, The Three Sikis, Barbara Sumner, Lorna Dean.
- 1957-58, *Puss In Boots:* Ken Barnes, Bonnie Downs, Patricia Vivian, Donald Stewart.
- 1958-59, *Dick Whittington:* Ronnie Hilton, Sonny Jenks, Billy Stutt, Don Arrol, Susan Swinford, Derek Westlake.
- 1959-60, *Jack and the Beanstalk:* Ken Dodd, Tony Heaton, Lisbeth Lennon.
- 1960-61, *Robin Hood:* John Hanson, Jimmy Wheeler, Freddie Frinton, Joe Baker, Jack Douglas.
- 1961-62, *Puss In Boots:* Tommy Cooper, George Bolton, Joy Turpin, Diana Day.
- 1962-63, *The Frog Prince:* Charlie Cairoli, Freddie Frinton, Billy Dainty, Astra Blair.
- 1963-64, *The Pied Piper of Hamelin:* Reg Varney, Freddie Sales, Joe Church, Terry Feris.
- 1964-65, *Tom Thumb:* Jimmy Clitheroe, Hope and Keen, Kathleen West, Danny Purches.
- 1965-66, *Robin Hood:* Mike and Bernie Winters, George Lacy, Michael Bevis, Manetti Twins, Ruth Evans.
- 1966-67, *Cinderella:* Freddie Frinton, Derek Dene, Kathleen West, Betty Jumel, Ruth Evans, John Larson.
- 1967-68, *The Pied Piper of Hamelin:* Freddy Davies, Mark Wynter, Don Smoothley, Betty Emery, Anna Lou and Maria.
- 1968-69, *Merry King Cole:* Harry Worth, Peter Butterworth, Lauri Lupino Lane, Robert Earl, Ann Harriman.
- 1969-70, *Dick Whittington:* Vince Hill, Bobby Dennis, Don Maclean, Don Smoothley, Toni-Sue Birley.
- 1970-71, *Robinson Crusoe:* Tommy Trinder, Jack Tripp, Marion Grimaldi, Allen Christie, Cox Twins, Miles Twins.
- 1971-72, *Cinderella:* John Hanson, David Hamilton, Wendy Bowman, Tommy Rose.
- 1972-73, *Aladdin:* Bobby Bennett, Jack Tripp, Jasmine Dee, June Shand.
- 1973-74, *Puss In Boots:* Freddie Garrity, Frankie Desmond, Terri Howard, Arthur Tolcher.
- 1974-75, *Jack and the Beanstalk:* Charlie Drake, Jack Smethurst, Nat Jackley, Cannon and Ball, Patsy Maclean.
- 1975-76, *Goldilocks and the Three Bears:* Terry Scott, Anne Aston, Jackie Pallo, Blayne Barrington.
- 1976-77, *Aladdin:* Barbara Windsor, Freddie Davies, Michael Bates, Donald Hewlett, Michael Knowles, John Clegg.
- 1977-78, *Cinderella:* Charlie Drake, Dora Bryan, Bernard Bresslaw, Bill Simpson, Anne Aston, Joe Black.
- 1978-79, *Babes In The Wood:* Les Dawson, Tammy Jones, Peter Goodwright, Ray Barraclough, Eli Woods.
- 1979-80, *Dick Whittington:* Bill Maynard, Alan Curtis, McDonald Hobley, Joy Launor-Heyes.
- 1980-81, *Jack and the Beanstalk:* Cannon and Ball, Norman Collier, Susan Maughan.
- 1981-82, *Aladdin:* Little and Large, Norman Collier, Patsy Ann Scott, Dudley Long.
- 1982-83, *Cinderella:* Russ Abbot, Denise Nolan, Dustin Gee, Les Dennis, Blayne Barrington.
- 1983-84, *Babes In The Wood:* The Krankies, Billy Dainty, Peter Goodwright, Alan Curtis, Janet Edis.
- 1984-86, Closed for refurbishment.
- 1986-87, *Babes In The Wood:* Cannon and Ball, Wyn Calvin, Craig Douglas.
- 1987-88, *Aladdin:* Sue Pollard, Jimmy Cricket, Paul Shane, Eli Woods, Jane Danielle, Joe Black, Maurice Thorogood.
- 1988-89, *Dick Whittington:* The Krankies, Christopher Biggins, Amanda Redington, Simon Bowman, Derek Holt, Russel Lane, Maurice Thorogood, Abigail Lee.

Note: From 1902-3 until 1929-30, and also 1933-34, the pantomimes were performed at the Prince's Theatre. From 1930-31 to date (except 1933-34), they were performed at the Alhambra Theatre.

But it was his 1940-41 *Aladdin* which proved the most historic of his pantomimes at the Coliseum. Starring Jean Colin, Iris Sadler and Jerry Verno (of *Taxi* fame), it was the only show which ran for weeks at the height of the London blitz — apart from that at the "We Never Closed" Windmill Theatre. Laidler at the time slept in the corridor of a bomb-damaged building.

"We never missed a performance", he recalled. "Often the audience could not leave at curtain-fall when the alert was still on, and so we used to 'ring up' again and put on an improvised entertainment, perhaps until two or three in the morning.

"I remember once the dame, Iris Sadler, well known to Bradford audiences, was singing a topical song about the air-raid shelters. At the exact moment when a drum-beat representing a bomb had to punctuate her song, a real block-buster fell quite near. She carried on and got a laugh out of her perfect timing".

They were anxious times for Francis Laidler though. The studios in Lambeth, where the scenery had been painted, were partly demolished by an air-raid before the work was fully completed. He managed to save most of the scenery, however, and found storage room at the Coliseum. "From then on," he said, "every day when I was going to the theatre I used to look eagerly up to see if the big globe, a familiar landmark, was still there. One night a big bomb fell through into the basement, but by amazing luck it was a dud. Its fall, however, damaged some of the scenery again and put all the stage machinery out of action, including the revolving stage apparatus. However, we managed by building a special platform and pushing the chorus on to the stage from the wings."

Steps to Fame or Fortune

The number of Francis Laidler's panto discoveries for whom the 'governor' provided a first step to loftier things is exceptional. He didn't neglect native talent either, but was a keen supporter of it. Some of the names may not ring a loud bell today, but they meant much in their time and others are still well known.

There was Yeadon comic, Sydney Howard, for example. He went on to become a West End celebrity and film star. Silly Billy Elliott also became famous as did John E. Coyle who triumphed in the record run of *Worm's Eye View*. Mona Vivian was quite a youngster when she first appeared for Laidler, while Bobbie Macauley went on to become the Bobby of Nat Mills and Bobbie.

Frank Robinson of the Eccleshill pantomimes found distinction and Mamie Watson became a musical comedy star. Margery Wyn also saw her name in lights in the West End.

Leslie Barker toured for a long time as partner to Gabrielle Ray, one of the most famous of all musical-stars, who also played principal girl in Bradford for Francis Laidler. Harry Thornton was a well known local vocalist and local too was Bessie Pratt, who was to be a much admired Alhambra principal girl. Fay Lenore and Rosaland Melville quickly made headway in musical comedy, and Percy Garside went on to become one of the most popular stalwarts of the Laidler pantos.

As for the Sunbeams, there were, in addition to Pat Paterson, who was to become a Hollywood star and wife of Charles Boyer, Mamie Souter, who made a name in Variety, and Mary O'Hare, who became a Bradford pantomime star. Ray and Zack, a successful Variety act, met in a Laidler pantomime when the girl known as Zack was a Sunbeam.

In addition to the 'unknowns' who were given a chance by Francis Laidler, there were of course scores of already established performers, many of whom, thanks to him, became even more celebrated.

Others left Laidler shows to marry well, including Nora Delaney, who became the wife of Prince Littler and Cora Goffin who became Mrs. Emile Littler. Some married well and still stayed on the stage, like Roma Beaumont who became the wife of impresario Alfred Black.

Many of the Laidler principal boys came into the spotlight, including Grace Draper, Viki Emra (partnered by the superb principal girl Jasmine Dee), Neta Underwood, Patricia Burke, Doreen Duke, Zena Dell and lovely Joy Beattie who married locally. The one Francis Laidler most helped to become renowned was probably Margery Manners — with the exception, of course, of his second wife, Gwladys.

Margery, who appeared numerous times in Laidler pantomimes at the Alhambra and the Theatre Royal, Leeds, was not only seductively glamorous, but she had a force of personality which brought back memories of the days when principal boys made as strong an impact as the leading comedians. Audiences were bewitched by her at the Alhambra, where she filled her dressing-room with masses of artificial flowers ("I like to see the place decorative") and dozens of dolls of all kinds ("A keen hobby of mine"). Quite a number of the dolls had been given to Margery by stage colleagues who found working with her such a happy experience.

As for snooker fans who rush to the small screen whenever Steve Davis, Hurricane Higgins or Bradford's Joe Johnson is in contest, they were beaten to interest in the game by Margery long ago. In her Laidler days she was already a skilled player, carrying a cue with her wherever she went. She had played snooker since childhood and didn't shy from a challenge from even the best of men players.

Margery went on to be a big hit of some of the *Good Old Days* TV programmes from the Leeds City Varieties when her impersonation of one of the greatest principal boys of old, Florrie Forde, was magnificent. It was appropriate too, for Florrie had been more than once a principal boy for Francis Laidler.

Born in Melbourne, Australia, Florrie Forde came to England in 1897 and made her first appearance in Bradford at the Empire in 1899. Five years later she topped the bill at the same theatre on the very night that the Alhambra opened just across the road. It was Florrie who introduced *Tipperary* which a year later was being sung by the 1914 B.E.F. as they landed in France, and she popularised *Anybody Here Seen Kelly?* and *Down at the Old Bull and Bush*.

Her own favourite song, however, was *Good-Bye-ee*. Ironically, she sang it in April 1940 as a final encore to patients in a naval hospital. Afterwards she collapsed in a car on the way back to Aberdeen where she was due to appear, and died a few hours later. Bradford was particularly sad because more than once Florrie had said it was "like home" to her. She had played to Alhambra audiences and she never supported the oft-heard complaint that they were hard to please. "They are quick on the up-take," she said, "and generous".

Randle's Scandals

In early January 1939, oblivious of the freeze outside and the accumulating war clouds, a scruffy old man in hiking shorts, with pack on back, walking pole in one hand and a bottle of swiftly vanishing Tizer in the other, was burping and belching on the Alhambra pantomime stage with the wind of the abandoned.

As I roared with mirth, my mother at one side, and her sister at the other, simultaneously elbowed me and demanded: "What are YOU laughing at?"

They were stoney-faced and offended by such "an outrageous exhibition" of erupting gases. Yet I noted that a good half of that packed audience, especially its younger members, were shrieking with hilarity.

And when the hiker told his next story they almost collapsed. In the fruity, slurred voice of a well-lubricated ancient, he related how he had been in a pub when nature called. But before he went outside, to be separated from his yet hardly drunk pint, he stuck a protective little notice on the glass. It warned: "I 'ave spit in this beer!" When he came back, someone had added: "So 'ave I!"

In those more dainty days, the audacious vulgarity of it all was astonishing. Nevertheless, it was a vulgarity more akin to the playground than to the salacious repartee of the customers of the men-only bar.

For all his chasing chorus girls across the stage with cries of "By gow, I bet tha's a 'ot 'un!" or "By gow, a'll waarm thee!" Wigan-born Frank Randle was not a comic of sexual sordidness. You had to be licentiously sly or sheer filthy to be that. And Frank was neither, in spite of all the times he was temporarily banished from the theatres of the North (during most of his career the South wouldn't touch him). He was just vigorously rude — yet, harmlessly funny with it.

Reputed to have been the only performer of his generation banned from Blackpool Central Pier, where the ladies in the holiday audiences were often broad-hipped mill lasses with even broader minds, Frank had an anarchic zest which was years ahead of its time. His wispy-haired, half-bald 'Old Hiker', and his "Any more for sailin'?" longshoreman, plus his "Get off mi fooit fatha!" catch phrase, would not only have earned him a fortune today, but would have won him many honours of his profession.

Ken Dodd once told me: "Frank was the funniest man I have ever seen. Max Miller might have so impressed his peers with the brilliance of his technique and timing that there was never anyone in the dressing-rooms when he was on stage. They all stood in the wings watching him and learning. But Frank was still the funniest."

In January 1939, however, when even such an innocuous word as 'damn' was much frowned on by 'decent people', there were thousands who wouldn't have agreed with Ken's assertion, believing that Randle was as bad as his word.

Consequently it was all the more amazing that Francis Laidler, who demanded 'good taste' from every other artist he ever booked, should engage Frank Randle to star as The Old Vizier in his 1938-39 *Aladdin* panto in which the gifted comedienne Iris Sadler played Widow Twankey and Peggy Bedell the title role.

Frank was not even particularly well known then (although he soon would be because of the attention the panto brought him). And Laidler must have been aware of his stage vulgarity because Frank had already appeared more than once in front of the much less narrow-minded Bradford Palace audiences.

Mr. Laidler never was to say why he selected Randle; so the choice was even more remarkable when you remember that Francis's morality rules for his stages was so strict that he didn't let even these lines pass in his 1914-15 Bradford pantomime:

> Where did you get that girl?
> Oh! you lucky devil.
> Where did you get that girl?
> Tell me on the level.

I have Francis's copy of the rehearsal script, and in pencil he deleted the words 'devil' and 'on the level' and added his own changes so that this is what audiences heard:

> Where did you get that girl?
> Oh! you lucky bounder.
> Where did you get that girl?
> Tell me where you found her.

In spite of the mystery, it's my conviction that Francis Laidler was such a perceptive man-of-the-theatre that, if he felt it merited it, he would put his own stage principles second. I am certain he picked Frank because he realised Randle's comic genius was so great that it demanded to be promoted.

Although at the Alhambra Frank didn't smash-up his dressing-room or bombard the audience with insults, and he was to do these later at other theatres, Frank did have words with Mr. Laidler during the run of Aladdin. And it was even admitted he was "proving rather difficult." But somehow all was smoothed over; and later Mr. Laidler didn't even hesitate in booking Frank's own show, *Randle's Scandals*, for the Alhambra.

Off-stage, Frank (1900-1957), who more than once ran into censorship wrangles with the Lord Chamberlain's office, was a dapper man, and his smart suits were far removed from the eccentricities of his stage outfits and thick make-up. But even in immaculate dress he could be an odd 'un.

Five years before his too early death he was, I recall, charged in Blackpool with driving while under the influence of drink. The ensuing court case was revealing and Randlesquely funny.

Giving evidence on his own behalf, he said that at the time of the alleged offence he was presenting a summer pier show, and proceedings were pending with regard to an unlicensed script. Summonses had been issued.

On the night in question the show ended at 11 p.m. and after that, up to 4.45 a.m., he worked on the script with his stage director and manager. During the show he had six to eight bottles of Guinness, and later three more, and a large gin.

Leaving the theatre in his car shortly after 5 a.m., he drove along the side of the Promenade and turned into Lytham Road, taking a wide sweep to avoid any traffic that might be coming from a side street. Then he felt a jar and his car went to the right. There was a tram, with one light on, in Lytham Road. He could not avert a collision.

His car, he said, scraped along the side of the tram and stalled. Later a policeman released his car door.

Frank continued: "The tram driver said, 'This man has been drinking.' I (Randle) asked him to repeat 'The Leith police dismisseth us, truly rurally, regularly ... and 'Good morning to Eve said Adam; good morning, sir, to him she said.'

"The tram driver said, 'What the --- are you talking about?' The driver seemed to get slightly annoyed. He said: 'I will punch you in the stomach'."

A hospital consultant, who had examined Randle, told the court that he found him "a compound of a queer mixture of things." His reactions were extraordinarily sharp. If Randle were drawing a gun, he would be quicker than anybody — but he might shoot the wrong person!

"I'n't it grand when yer daft"

The above phrase was his rallying call for more than half a century. And the joyous simplicity of his creed, upon which he never permitted anything blue or suggestive to infringe, made Albert Modley more than admired by the Alhambra panto and Variety audiences who wiped away the tears of laughter tickled out of them by his 'gormless' and often flat-capped antics and daft yarns. Those audiences loved him.

Albert, who learned his trade in the pubs and clubs before Francis Laidler helped him on his way to become a star of nearly thirty pantos and scores of summer shows and radio and TV presentations, once said: "When I started being a comic the lads thought at first I was from the Band of Hope. But they laughed just the same and soon decided it was all right to bring the missus and kids to the club that night. That's how we packed them in".

In the days when the BBC insisted on vetting the scripts of comedians who were to broadcast, it made an exception in Albert's case. It trusted him completely and never requested a look at his material. As for Francis Laidler, his trust in Albert was complete.

Albert once said: "The beauty of it is that clean comedy floors them. They have got so used to swear words nowadays that when they hear a bit of clean comedy they don't know what's struck them. When you get people laughing away with their handkerchiefs out to dab their eyes, that's marvellous. That's real humour. All simple stuff."

His humour had an innocent, trusting, child-like, but never childish, quality which zestfully looked upon life as fun — a game, a lark, a prank in which anyone taking themselves too seriously deserved to be banished from the arena.

In Albert's book nothing was meant to be taken too seriously. He had been born with a grin on his face, he insisted. And he didn't care about age. He was seventy-seven when he died in 1979 at his home in Morecambe where he had lived for many years, helping to bring so much joy to the resort that he was given the Freedom of the Town.

Although born in Liverpool, Albert came across the Pennines as a young lad and considered himself a Yorkshireman by adoption. He lived for a considerable period in the Ilkley area. Before turning professional comedian he worked in the parcels office at Forster Square Railway Station, Bradford, and he reckoned that when he went into show business full time, it was the station's gain.

His kindness was renowned. For example, during the run of one of the Alhambra's most successful pantomimes he sent flowers to the girl programme-sellers and the female bar staff every week. And for the backstage lads he made sure a barrel of ale was on tap for them in the wings throughout the run. "There were nowt daft about that", remembered one of them. "It was typical of that luverly man."

Over the Skyscraper Wall

In 1949 a former commercial traveller of Rochdale, who had worked in a cotton mill when he was fourteen, walked along New York's Broadway and said to himself as he looked up at those formidable, unfriendly skyscrappers: "Well, Norman. I don't think you've much of a chance here lad."

He was wrong, as it turned out. For that night he entertained a cheering audience and awoke next morning to read in the *Herald-Tribune* that "He smashed the audience to smithereens". Picking up the *Journal-American* he found that Robert Garland was informing New Yorkers, "You'll never find his equal", while the great Brooks Atkinson of the *New York Times* was hailing him as "the one genuine vaudeville performer on the bill".

Norman Evans, who with much trepidation had made an "experimental trip" to America was wowing the States with the same basic *Over the Wall* sketch which Alhambra audiences had deliriously applauded only a few months before, in the 1948-49 pantomime, *Red Riding Hood*.

The Alhambra had already known many fine panto dames (like Bertram Dench and Bunny Doyle) and were to know more (Jack Storey and Rob Currie for example), but Norman was the incomparable companion.

His first panto for Francis Laidler in Bradford was the 1943-44 *Humpty-Dumpty* in which that delightful mighty atom, Betty Jumel, took the title role. During wartime

ALHAMBRA THEATRE

BRADFORD

Thursday December 23rd and Friday December 24th, at 5.30
One Performance on Christmas Day at 2 o'clock, and afterwards

TWICE DAILY AT 1.30 AND 5.30

FRANCIS LAIDLER'S

Entirely New and Magnificent Comedy Pantomime

HUMPTY DUMPTY

NORMAN EVANS " Martha "

A SUPERB PRODUCTION

LAUGHTER ALL THE TIME

Norman Evans as 'Martha' in Humpty Dumpty,
one of his great Alhambra triumphs, 1943-44

Norman Evans brought such a spirit-elevating feast of fun to the Alhambra stage that the word got around faster than bullets. Consequently box-office queues stretched way up Morley Street.

A great strength of Norman Evans was that he was never one of those 'glamorous' dames who are half-way to being drag artists. His dame was unashamedly working-class and asexual, with carbolic-scrubbed, rosy-apple cheeks, beefy biceps and neat workaday dresses so crisp and clean that a farmer's wash-tub-loving wife would have been proud to hang them on her line. When Norman's dame complained about the cat falling into the Yorkshire pudding mixture you felt certain that not only could 'she' really make Yorkshire pudding, but that 'she' could make the best Yorkshire pudding in the universe.

Norman Evans's *Over the Wall* sketch, involving an imaginery neighbour, superbly burlesqued the gossiping across the fences of a million ordinary terraces. And his dentist sketch, in which he played the tooth-yanker while a make-believe patient behind a screen went through the torments of Hades, transcended everything as it turned a universal terror into a riot of laughter.

In checkered dustcap, with glasses slipped down to the end of his nose and with an ear-to-ear pulled-in, upturned mouth, Norman gave us a Mother Hubbard-like dame who sucked in the tittle-tattle of her world only to spout it out later like a blowing whale. And Norman's dame *was* a whale of a performance.

As an amateur, Norman had been encouraged to become a professional entertainer by an 'old girl' of his hometown, Gracie Fields, and he soon made it — right up to a Royal Command Variety performance. Nevertheless, it was Francis Laidler who absorbed him into pantomime and helped transform him into possibly the best dame since Dan Leno.

In 1955 Norman lost an eye in a car crash, although it was announced that he had recovered quickly. Not long afterwards, however, he was not the same. Much of the zest and sparkle had gone and he had to rely too much on the little toy panda which had long been a minor feature of his act. By December 1962 he was dead. He was sixty-one, but destined to live for many more years in any history of all-time pantomime greats.

The Good and Bad New Days

In April 1936 the Alhambra's bill-posters announced:

SANDY POWELL
The Popular Comedian
with his
1936 ROAD SHOW
See Sandy In His New Sketches
The Broadcasting Studio At The
Stage Door

It was a significant announcement because its reference to broadcasting told some of the story of Variety at the time — and heralded a lot of it later. The wireless, as everyone called radio then, was beginning to take off in a big way and it was only natural that listeners wanted to see some of the broadcasters in person.

Early on, however, radio didn't seem too interested in Variety, apparently looking at it down the refined noses of the B.B.C.'s top brass. But inevitably it crept in, even if some of the outside broadcasts from theatres were a bit farcical, to say the least. One-wheel cyclists and jugglers, for instance, were hardly appropriate material for the air.

By 1936, though, Variety entertainers were becoming sufficiently established wireless personalities to warrant radio being spotlighted in theatre billings. Not that theatre managements were too happy about it. Originally they had been up in arms when they saw radio as a rival threatening to take away their best talent. After all, they argued, who would want to come to their theatres and pay to see entertainers who they could hear for nothing at home?

How wrong they were! As more and more entertainers toured as radio luminaries, more and more people clamoured to see in person those whose voices had enthralled them when they gathered round their sets.

Some of those entertainers were already Variety performers, but they had been a long way from becoming household names before broadcasting became popular. Radio had

BRADFORD
ALHAMBRA

Managing Director - Francis Laidler

BOOKED IN CONJUNCTION WITH MOSS' EMPIRES Ltd.

6-30   Twice Nightly   8-40

*Every Seat in the House can be booked
in Advance without any extra charge.*

PRICE 2D.

Cover of a 1935 programme

made them stars and everybody wanted to see them in the flesh. This was even more so when the second world war broke out and the imaginery missus of Robb Wilton, one of the funniest men I have ever seen at the Alhambra, asked him her now immortal question: What was he going to do about it?

The wireless was a priceless comfort and buffer against Hitler's murderous insanities and many were those who played the Alhambra who had been heard in such radio classics as *Garrison Theatre* and *Saturday Night Music Hall* — a much-loved title, even if true Music Hall had been deposed by Variety years before.

Jack ("Mind my bike!") Warner (later of *Dock Green* fame); Old Mother Riley and her stage daughter Kitty; Nat Mills and Bobbie; Will Hay; Suzette Tarri; Elsie and Doris Waters (sisters of Jack Warner) with their perky Cockney characters, Gert and Daisy; the drawling-voiced Western Brothers, comic toffs at the piano; Gillie ("Wake up England!") Potter, Flanagan and Allen; Claude Dampier, of goofish aspect; and double-act drolls Clapham and Dwyer (made by radio) were but a few who starred at the Alhambra and, on wireless, eased the pains of war.

Thanks to the brilliance of scriptwriter Ted Kavanagh, wartime radio was to be responsible for changing the concept of comedy. Kavanagh's ITMA (*It's That Man Again*), with Liverpool comedian Tommy Handley superbly spearheading the fun, hilariously turned reality on its head in a fantasy world of blissful lunacy, as well as giving the nation such enduring catchphrases as "Don't Forget the Diver", "This is Funf Speaking" and, of course, Mrs. Mopp's evergreen "Can I Do You Now, Sir?" Throughout the war Tommy led a captivating team of comic and fantastic montebanks in a weekly verbal rough-and-tumble in which anything could happen — and usually did.

When those who claimed in the 1950's that The Goons had completely revoluntionised comedy with their inspired absurdities, they had forgotten that ITMA was the true pathfinder for the illogicalities of that Comedy of the Ridiculous which is still favoured today.

Tommy Handley, who died in 1949 at the age of fifty-five, became a superstar, thanks to radio, but he was still a long way from that when he appeared at the Alhambra as Mr. Winterbottom of the Mr. Murgatroyd and Mr. Winterbottom double-act with Ronald Frankau, a smoothly debonair comedian. The Alhambra saw Tommy too in the crazy upheaval of *The Disorderly Room,* a sketch which ran off and on from 1920 to 1941. It was toured for Leslie Henson for whom Tommy did concert party work.

Tommy transferred comfortably to radio, but there were many others who didn't. They included one of the best of the old-time comics, Harry Tate, who sported a huge, waggly imitation moustache similar to the one worn by one of the most legendary of Alhambra favourites, Billy Bennett ("boom-boom").

Harry, one of whose catchphrases was "How's your father?" (you still hear it today), made his first appearance as a comic at the Oxford Music Hall, London, in 1895 and became famous for his sporting sketches, especially the one about early motoring, which he played no less than 15,000 times. Alhambra audiences laughed till they cried at the visual havoc caused by Harry's incompetence, but, alas, such havoc was hardly suitable for radio.

Nevertheless, radio decided it wanted Harry. He agreed to go to the studio, but didn't much care for the experience. Consequently, the next time he was invited Harry, who was sixty-seven when he died in 1940, took along his big false moustache and wore it throughout the broadcast. He did the same thing for every subsequent broadcast — even if his waggling of the moustache at the microphone, unseen by the listening and unaware millions, had a pathos which illustrates all too clearly how harsh radio's demands could be on some of the older giants of Variety.

The Sandy Man

Sandy Powell's Alhambra sketch about radio went down well. One reviewer spoke for all his colleagues when he wrote: "Sandy's famous Test Match sketch was, as always, refreshing; but he was at his best as the man who refused to be quiet in a broadcasting studio".

And Powell knew all about broadcasting studios. In 1928 his *Sandy's Hour* became the first ever regular BBC Variety show on the wireless and it continued, under various names, for many years.

That radio gave Sandy the honour of being first is not difficult to understand. In my view he was the complete entertainer and comedian of his time — just as much at home on radio as he was on records and on the stage, and was later to be in films and on television. If there was ever a performer who was a true professional, it was Sandy — a 'pro' to his fingertips.

What's more, as the BBC appreciated immediately, he was 'safe'. During a career which stretched from the age of five (he borrowed an older cousin's birth certificate to fool the licensing people so that he could appear on his mother's marionette show) until his death at eighty-two in 1982 he never told a smutty joke. Like Albert Modley he gusted through Variety and everything else he did on a joy of innocent laughter.

Sandy, who coined his catchphrase, "Can you hear me, mother?", on radio, appeared many times at the Alhambra but never, surprisingly, in pantomime. "I did play for Francis Laidler at the Theatre Royal, Leeds, though," he once told me. "I was just out of my teens when he engaged me as a page in *Cinderella*."

Sandy, whose ventriloquist sketch was a comic gem for decades, was born in Rotherham. As a child he had it rough and tough. His stagehand father, over-fond of the bottle and the girls, upped and went, leaving his mother, who had retired as a not over successful Variety artist, to return to the halls in order to pay the bills. Even as a toddler Sandy was studying some of the stars from the wings.

He made his first paid professional appearance in 1909 at Keighley, as the nine-year-old assistant of a stage mesmerist. As a youngster he "played all the big 'cities' like Pudsey, Morley and Batley," and was appearing at Yeadon Town Hall at the time of his thirteenth birthday.

His first appearance in Bradford was at the Towers Hall in Manchester Road, as a "lantern-cooler" as Variety acts in cinemas were then called. His first big break came at the Dewsbury Empire when 'Wee' Georgie Wood, who was starring there, fell ill. Sandy, who was appearing at the City Varieties, Leeds, was asked to take over. He never looked back.

Towards the end of his life he did have one complaint, though. "So many young artists nowadays," he said, "all seem to sound alike. They sing the same songs, have the same mannerisms. We tried to be individuals, to be different."

All of Sandy's heroes certainly had been different — Marie Lloyd, Little Titch, Harry Weldon and (a great favourite of his) Hetty King — and few entertainers have been more individual than Sandy Powell himself.

Jessie, Two Henrys, and a Gracie

She made her last Alhambra stage entrance in a Bradford mill skep, but there wasn't a member of the audience who didn't know that the smell of raw wool was as foreign to her as were the aromas of Soho to a West Riding loom-minder.

In fact the slim, pretty lady with the tip-tilted nose, saucer eyes of china blue and radiant smile *had* been born in Soho — in Berwick Street, on March 11th 1907 — and she was still a proud Londoner from the toes of her high-kicking feet to her straight fringe and the big bow on top of her fascinating little head.

Alhambra audiences forgave her those origins. In fact they would have forgiven her anything. For she was Jessie Matthews who, in the 1940's was still the singing and dancing darling of revue and musical comedy.

Long before she had seven million listeners tuning in faithfully to *Mrs. Dale's Diary,* in which she played the title role for six years in more than 1,500 episodes, Jessie was the toast of the capital, then of the whole country and finally of America. As late as 1979, when she appeared in concert in the States, she was rapturously received by Hollywood — for she had been a film star too.

During that 'mill skep' visit, Jessie was accompanied to the Alhambra by her second husband, Sonnie Hale, and she was quick to tell him how important this theatre was to her. For it was her appearance in a revue at the Alhambra in the mid-twenties that really put her on the road to overnight fame in London in an Andre Charlot show. So tumultuous had been the applause at the Alhambra that the West End just had to sit up and take notice.

Jessie, famous for such songs as *Dancing on the Ceiling* and *My Heart Stood Still* — both written for her by the great Richard Rodgers and Lorenz Hart — also reminded Sonnie that when the Charlot revue went to New York it was given the 'bird'. "They threw pennies to us," she admitted. "How could anyone be conceited after that?"

Jessie's first husband had been Henry Lytton Jnr., son of Sir Henry Lytton, comic supremo of the D'Oyly Carte Opera Company and the Gilbert and Sullivan operas. Henry Jnr. had himself been the star of numerous musicals when he appeared at the Alhambra in the 1962-63 pantomime. They included *Hit the Deck, The Girl Friend* and *West End Scandals.*

His reminiscences about his father, who bewitched Alhambra audiences, were eye-opening. Sir Henry, it appeared, could not read music and had to be taught every note of the operas by ear. But he saw to it that his family had a firm musical training.

"My father was a Victorian martinet," said Henry Lytton Jnr, "a keen disciplinarian. Everything in the household had to move with clockwork precision. At lunchtime, if we children were late and the meat course had been served, we had to do without it and subsist on sweet and dessert. If we did not open the door for father or mother there was blue murder in the atmosphere."

Nevertheless, Sir Henry's children were fond of him. "He had a wonderful sense of fun", said his son. "It could flabbergast an audience and alarm the D'Oyly Carte management. For example, he and I looked very much alike, so on one occasion, for a jest, he played Ko-Ko during the first act (of *The Mikado*) and had me playing Ko-Ko during the second act. No one realised it until the finale when two Ko-Kos stepped on stage to take their bow!"

Henry Jnr. told me that during all the years with D'Oyly Carte his father never received more than £60 a week. "Of course, you have to remember that he was employed for fifty-two weeks a year and that £60 was worth quite a lot then. Nevertheless, there were others getting a lot more at the time."

One performer at least was certainly getting a great deal more. During the 1930's when, like Sir Henry Lytton, she had the Alhambra audiences spellbound, 'Our Gracie', the Lancashire lass from Rochdale who started her career at a shilling a week, was earning up to £15,000 a year.

Many marvellous advancements were still to happen in the life of Gracie Fields when she starred at the Alhambra, but audiences soon appreciated her genius, as did the managements with their ready cheque books. The diamond buckles on her shoes bore witness to that.

Her genius endured. Nine years before she died in 1973, aged eighty-one, she returned from her sunny retirement on the Isle of Capri to star at the Batley Variety Club. She was so electrifying that she received a standing ovation from the cheering audience, including the Press. Club owner James Corrigan exclaimed: "She was fantastic. She lost forty years when she was on stage."

After the show, during which she sang contemporary songs as well as many she had made famous, like *Sally, Little Old Lady, Sing as we Go* and *The Biggest Aspidistra in the World,* Gracie told me that although she had had standing ovations during overseas tours it was the first time she had ever had one in Britain.

When she came to the Alhambra in the thirties, Gracie's Rochdale upbringing was still vivid in her mind and the following memories of her youth are not only evocative in themselves, but give some idea of how Variety in those days was one of the few escape routes to fame and fortune for gifted working-class girls.

"I started when I was seven," she said, "singing from the gallery to a woman on stage. I was determined to be an actress — no, it didn't run in the family; nobody else had ever done it. Then I played in a troupe for a shilling a week. We did half-an-hour and I was twenty minutes of it.

"I never really went to school. At twelve they gave me a comic number to do. When the audience laughed, I cried. I thought they had no right to laugh — and me with a voice like Patti's — and I wanted to be a turn on my own. I was fourteen and full of myself, with a head the size of six, and I wouldn't take under £5 a week.

"I stuck it out and at last I got it. I deputised for somebody, but it didn't last and I couldn't keep up to my £5 level. I joined a concert party — what a come-down I thought it! It was quite by accident I became a comedienne. I mimicked members of the company and when people like Gertie Gitana were on the bill I imitated them for mother and the people on our street ...

"Not getting enough work, my mother said I must go to the mill like other girls. Cotton mill, shop, paper-bag factory — I did all sorts of things for two years. I wore clogs — I've still got 'em, size fives. My mother was pushing me on to the stage with one hand and pulling me off with the other.

"At sixteen I joined a revue. Mother said if I didn't make good there I should have to return to the mill for good. I dreaded the mill and knew I'd rather do anything than go back. But my luck turned — thank God."

When Gracie Fields, whose voice shamed some opera singers, appeared at the Alhambra in 1931 she was invited to a charity dinner-dance at the new Victoria Ballroom. Present were six youngsters who were keen members of the children's club which annually staged its own revue in Bradford. Those youngsters presented Gracie with a little gnome-faced badge and made her an honorary Nignog.

A Little Wiseman

The word 'Nignog' has been regarded, inaccurately, by some people as a derogatory term, but it is actually derived from the German *nicht* and the French *noblesse* and means simply 'not of the nobility'. It was coined by the children of French aristocrats brought up at Coblenz during the revolution.

In the 1930's, however, and for many years afterwards it was the much esteemed title of a children's club run by Bradford's *Telegraph & Argus* newspaper. Hundreds of youngsters from Bradford and its environs became Nignogs and were proud of it. The club's yearly stage revues were strongly supported, but one of them was to prove more significant than usual. On Tuesday, March 31st 1936, this notice appeared in the Telegraph & Argus:

> "An audience of nearly 2,000, applauding with enthusiasm and vigour, marked the presentation at the Bradford Alhambra last night of the Telegraph & Argus Nignog Club's sixth annual revue. Nignog Revues in previous years have been responsible for discovering individual talent, and it would seem that among the newly-acquired players this year there is a real 'find'. He is Ernest Wiseman, a diminutive comedian who certainly has a way with him. It was a first appearance, yet he performed like an old-timer, and with such droll airs that the audience roared with laughter. The more they cheered, the more Ernest enjoyed it, and in his tiny bowler hat and check suit he made a wonderful hit ..."

The young comedian, whom the reviewer praised so perceptively, was to become half of one of the century's best comic double-acts. Yes, Ernest Wiseman was to grow up to be Ernie Wise whose partner Eric Morecambe would delight in pulling his cheek and demanding, "Who's a little Nignog then?"

"I still have all the programmes for the Alhambra revues I was in ," said Ernie nearly fifty years after that first notice. "The shows taught me so much. Before then I'd been going on the stage in the clubs with my dad, but the Leeds Education Authorities stopped that! I came over to Bradford to get round that order. Among the songs I remember singing were *I'm Knee Deep in Daisies* and *Let's Have a Tiddley at the Milkbar.*"

Ernie's Nignog revue successes brought him to the notice of Bryan Mickie of the BBC. After a successful audition he was recommended to Jack Hylton and the result was that in 1939 Ernie made his professional debut in the BBC *Band Wagon Show* at the Prince's Theatre, Shaftesbury Avenue, London.

Singing *The Lambeth Walk,* the youngster from the back-to-backs near Leeds won a tremendous ovation. "As you can see," said Ernie, "the Nignog revues and the Bradford Alhambra were very important parts of my life." He added. "I have just come back from Australia and I bet you don't realise how world-wide the affection is for the *Telegraph & Argus?* Even in Sydney, Perth and Adelaide people full of happy memories came up to me to say they used to be in the same Nignog children's club as I was."

Appropriately, Ernie Wise, accompanied by his delightful wife, was a guest of honour when the newly refurbished Alhambra opened its doors on Tuesday, May 27th 1986. In his lapel was the Nignog badge he had treasured all those years.

Jack the Wasp

Another look at the review of the Nignog show reveals that it includes another name which was to become renowned — that of Leslie Sands, a Bradford Hanson schoolboy who is now a prominent television actor as well as a gifted author and playwright.

Leslie, who, like Ernie, loved his young days at the Alhambra, was so upset in 1983 when he heard the theatre might have to close permanently, that he helped spearhead an appeal by stage folk to save it. "It would be absolutely tragic if the Alhambra closed," he said. "It is one of the most marvellous theatres in the country. It is not like those glass and concrete monstrosities which aren't really theatres at all. The irony of any closure talk is that if the Alhambra were kept open it would, in time, be a national monument."

In September 1972 Leslie helped bring to the Alhambra an exceptionally appealing production featuring a balanced and beautiful selection from the works of Bradford author and playwright, J. B. Priestley. It was presented to mark the writers seventy-eighth birthday and Priestley was there himself — although because of a temporary ailment he had to bring a cushion with him for comfort.

The production was called *The World of J. B. Priestley* and I mention it especially because, although not many people are aware of it, his world included a dramatic appearance on the Alhambra stage.

In his youth, of course, Jack Priestley had been an avid theatregoer in Bradford, falling particularly under the spell of Little Titch at the Empire, Jimmy Learmouth ("One of the best comedians I ever saw.") who played the Alhambra, and the straight-theatre touring companies at the Theatre Royal. He was also a keen pantomime fan — so much so that when he was eighty he wrote to me asking if I had any information about an actress who had been in panto at the Theatre Royal donkey's years ago (donkey's years to me anyway).

"I have a very clear recollection of Mabel Sealby as principal girl in the Theatre Royal pantomime," he wrote, "and I well remember she had a row with the management sometime about the middle of the run." (It transpired that Priestley had fallen in love with Mabel when he was a schoolboy — worshipping her from afar and never to meet her.)

The cause of J. B. Priestley's Alhambra appearance was the Beecham Opera Company. In the spring of 1919 Francis Laidler heard that the Beecham company was likely to have a fortnight to spare between visits to Manchester and London, so he tried to secure a visit to Bradford. Sir Thomas, however, would not hear of it, for he had no great regard for Bradford even then!

Laidler persisted and even offered to guarantee the expenses for a fortnight, but still Tommy Beecham would not agree to spend two weeks in Bradford. "For a week then," Laidler suggested, and he asked how large a sum would be required. It was a matter of thousands, but Laidler accepted the terms and a week's visit was arranged. He immediately started a publicity campaign and within a fortnight the guaranteed amount was reached in advance bookings.

He then wired: "What about the second week?" and the reply came, "With pleasure. No guarantee required."

It was this great success that induced the British National Opera Company to launch itself at the Alhambra in 1922 and to return for several years. Mind you, I don't think the British National Opera would have been much impressed by J. B. Priestley's contribution to the Beecham Opera Company's triumph — as he himself would have been the first to agree.

It was a practice by the Beecham company to recruit local supernumeraries for its productions and Jack Priestley was persuaded by a friend to be one of these walk-ons in Gounod's *Romeo and Juliet*. But after entering the stage door to don a yellow and black doublet, one black tight and one striped yellow and black tight, he looked, in his own words, "like a rather plump wasp."

He was not asked to appear again. "But then, on the other hand," he said, "I never asked to be asked again."

Beecham Thunder

Sir Thomas Beecham, with wit as pointed as a rapier, could be, when he chose, one of the great humorous men of the century. But he was also notoriously quarrelsome, insulting many of those who supported him although usually behaving afterwards as if nothing had happened.

His relationship with Bradford was for a long time a genuinely bitter one. Although he spent hundreds of thousands of pounds in furthering the cause of opera in this country, not one penny piece of his money was dropped in Bradford. He thought it musically backward — hence his original reluctance to bring the Beecham Opera Company to the Alhambra in 1919.

His reluctance then, however, was nothing compared with his anger on Monday night, November 12th 1935, when he conducted members of the Royal Opera House, Covent Garden, in a performance at the Alhambra of *Koanga* by Bradford-born Frederick Delius.

Beecham was Delius's greatest champion and the greatest interpreter of his music. "Delius is wonderfully gifted and destined to play perhaps the most important part in the development of modern music in England ... My prophecy — don't forget it!" he commanded.

Unfortunately most of Bradford remained unimpressed and behaved as if Delius didn't even exist. That didn't please Tommy Beecham at all and in a spirit of "I'll show 'em" he began his 1935 opera season at the Alhambra with a Delius work never before heard of in Bradford, let alone performed.

"Delius got remarkable poignancy from the story of a Negro's love for a fellow slave and her suicide over his body after he had been flogged to death," wrote the *Telegraph & Argus* critic next day when praising John Brownie and Olga Slobodskaya who sang the leading roles.

The critic also noted: "Sadder than the story of *Koanga* was the fact that not even under Beecham and with a first-class company did the performance of the Bradford composer's opera anywhere near fill the Alhambra. With this original work, written by Delius largely as the outcome of his sojourn in Florida, Sir Thomas Beecham's new opera company thus made its Yorkshire debut in circumstances that hardly rebound to the credit of the city."

Sir Thomas more than agreed. "It is questionable whether I shall ever return to this town," he thundered at a luncheon given to members of his company at Busby's department store in Manningham Lane.

Censuring in strong terms Bradford's lack of interest and appreciation of good opera, Sir Thomas said that *Koanga* had been presented in Manchester the previous week and had been very successful. "If a similar performance of a work by a great composer had been given in any town or city on the Continent," he insisted, "it would have been impossible to get a seat for love or money. The lack of appreciation shown last night at the Alhambra will go down in history as a black spot. I shall report this in the public Press at some length and in no uncertain terms. It was an insult to the memory of a great man."

Asked what his impression of the *Koanga* audience was, Sir Thomas said: "I have no impression, except that it was inadequate in numbers." He then pointed out that for a concert series he was to give in America it was impossible to get a seat for the next three years. "Why should I come to Bradford?" he asked. "I go to Berlin and you cannot get in. I go to America and you cannot get in. Here in Bradford we play a splendid work by my greatest friend and you do not come in. If I come to Bradford again I shall require some very serious evidence in advance that the public will support the operas."

In later years Beecham did return to Bradford many times, but he could never quite forgive its citizens' indifference to Delius. Yet his faith in the composer was eventually vindicated. In April 1962 Frederick was fully honoured by a Delius Centenary Festival attended by the Queen Mother and culminating in a performance by Sadler's Wells Opera of his *A Village Romeo and Juliet,* with John Wakefield and Elsie Morrison in the title roles. This time an ecstatic audience at the Alhambra was near capacity.

Opera and Musicals

One nationally respected critic wrote in his review of Delius's opera, *A Village Romeo and Juliet:* Of course the Alhambra has no adequate orchestra pit; a fact so self-evident that it hardly seems worth mentioning.''

He was right about that and he could have mentioned the inadequate size of the stage, too, for the Alhambra had been built with the less demanding needs of Variety in mind. Nevertheless, for years big opera and musical companies continued to struggle there until technical advancements became so colossal that the theatre couldn't accommodate them. Bradford was then by-passed by most of the *larger* companies.

However, until the final crunch came, and using great staging ingenuity, the Alhambra managed to present many operatic and musical productions which pleased the public.

The Carl Rosa Company, for example, was for a long time a regular visitor, featuring in *La Boheme* on one memorable occasion a spine-tingling tenor called Oreste Kirkop who went on to Hollywood to appear in the title role of *The Vagabond King.*

The D'Oyly Carte Opera company was a perennial Alhambra favourite almost from the start and John Reed, who brilliantly recreated the Gilbert and Sullivan roles made famous by Sir Henry Lytton, has now so many friends in the area that he directs, and appears in, some of the operas for the non-professional West Yorkshire Savoyards Appreciation Society which has toured America to acclaim.

The Sadler's Wells Opera Company, so large sometimes that one can only wonder how it coped backstage at the Alhambra, gave many fine performances to full houses of the great classics of opera, as well as lighter works such as *Die Fledermaus,* which was equally popular.

The Wells Company visit in September, 1960, was overshadowed by tragedy when its special train hit the buffers at Forster Square Station and eleven of its members were injured. One of them was sixty-three-year-old Jack Harvey, who had been a tenor with the company for more than thirty years.

He was taken to Bradford Royal Infirmary with shock, but soon afterwards insisted on leaving because of a rehearsal commitment. The same night he became ill and returned to the Infirmary where he died the following day. That week a moving musical tribute was paid to him by members of the company at St. John's Church, Little Horton. Members of the chorus sang part of the Pilgrim's chorus from *Tannhauser,* in which Jack was to have appeared at the Alhambra.

So many musicals have been presented at the Alhambra that it is possible to mention only a few of them here; but the following representative list should bring back memories:

Annie Get Your Gun, The Belle of New York, Bitter Sweet, Carousel, Chu Chin Chow, Careless Rapture, The Dancing Years, The Desert Song, A Funny Thing Happened on the Way to the Forum, Guys and Dolls, Hair, Lock up Your Daughters, Glamorous Night, Lady Be Good, Kiss Me, Kate, The Merry Widow, The New Moon, No, No, Nanette, Oklahoma!, Paint Your Wagon, Rose Marie, Rio Rita, Showboat, Sunny, The Sound of Music, The Student Prince, Wedding in Paris (a premiere), *White Horse Inn, Wild Violets* and *The Vagabond King.*

Of that list I have special regard for *Kiss Me, Kate, Carousel* and *Chu Chin Chow,* for in Elizabeth Larner, Edmund Hockridge and the Maori singer Inia Te Wiata respectively, the Alhambra had three of the finest leading players to grace its stage.

I am not forgetting John Hanson, of course, but he merits a place of his own in any story of the Alhambra. Again and again he brought musicals to this theatre when others either passed it by or insisted it had become too costly to take this kind of show on the road.

The Alhambra, where John also starred in pantomime, was one of his favourite dates — indeed, he thought so much of it that in 1966, before its London opening, he presented there his own musical, *When You're Young,* based on the popular play, *Smilin' Through.* It won much applause.

But like other theatres the Alhambra will remember John Hanson most for his 'Red Shadow' in *The Desert Song.* He played the part with a panache equalled only by Harry Welchman who created the role in 1927 and who also appeared at the Alhambra.

Ballet, Beautiful Ballet

Still considered by some to have been the greatest ballerina of the twentieth century, Anna Pavlova was in the wings of the Alhambra in October, 1930, preparing to dance yet again *The Dying Swan,* which was always in demand. This time, however, the dance was prophetic, for three months later, at the age of 49, she would be gone and her body lying in state at the Russian church in Buckingham Palace Road, London.

At the Alhambra there had been no sign that this daughter of a St. Petersburg laundress, was anything other than hale and hearty. With not the slightest suggestion of temperament she chatted animatedly with admirers and once more (although she must have been weary of it) *The Dying Swan* was cheered.

Pavlova became more than a living legend, for it was she whose art paved the way for a wider appreciation of ballet in Britain, as well as inspiring a small girl named Alice Marks, who years later was to be revered as Alicia Markova.

Markova herself became an Alhambra star with the Markova-Dolin Ballet when Anton Dolin thrilled audiences with the dance always demanded of him — Ravel's *Bolero.*

Until its stage was considered inadequate the Alhambra was regularly a home of ballet, featuring among companies there The Royal Ballet, Ballet Rambert, London Ballet, Metropolitan Ballet, International Ballet, Scottish Theatre Ballet and, of course, London Festival Ballet whose Beryl Grey has long been one of the warmest friends of the Alhambra.

In April 1968 the Alhambra experienced one of the great events of its history when, on a stage a sixth of the size of the ones they are accustomed to in their homeland, fourteen stars of the Russian Bolshoi and Kirov Ballets gave a performance which, as far as principal dancers are concerned, was in my opinion six times greater artistically than any ballet presentation previously seen in Bradford.

Nine years later, in December 1976, one of the most captivating and memorable pages was written into the Alhambra's history when Dame Margot Fonteyn appeared in an enchanting production of *Romeo and Juliet,* in which she was splendidly partnered by David Wall.

In many of the triumphs of her career Fonteyn was, of course, partnered by another genius of the ballet — Rudolf Nureyev — and it was much to the credit of the management of the refurbished Alhambra that it engaged him to dance with Northern Ballet Theatre not many days after it first opened its doors. On Monday, June 6th, 1986, therefore, there stepped on to the hugely extended stage the still spell-casting forty-eight-year-old dancer who was to say afterwards that he had been delighted to appear in a theatre as well-equipped as the Alhambra. It was a momentous night for the "new" Alhambra and its memory should become a legend of the new era.

Wartime Glitter

During the second World War the outside of the Alhambra was painted a dark chocolate brown as camouflage because of the danger of bombing. The theatre's exterior became a dreary sight, but inside, as had been the case only two decades before, it was a cheerful oasis where wartime anxieties and fears could be left outside — temporarily, anyway.

The Laidler policy was simple — to put up two fingers at Hitler and his gang in the shape of productions of jollity and, whenever possible, optimistic glitter. Not only did he succeed in this with some of his best pantomimes, but he brought a good deal of colourful spectacle to the Alhambra, plus some top artists who personified romance.

Three of these were particularly applauded — Ivor Novello, Richard Tauber and Carl Brisson.

Novello, creator of so many melodically and visually sumptuous musicals, arrived at the Alhambra in April 1941 to stage for a fortnight one of his greatest triumphs, *The Dancing Years,* as a happy antidote to the worries of war.

At the stage door he spotted a Bradford friend and said: "You see I have kept my promise." The undertaking had been made some years before when he was appearing at the Alhambra in a play called *The Rat.* It was decided that when he next came to the Alhambra he would bring Muriel Barron as his leading lady.

In the 1930's Muriel had been a member of the Bradford Amateur Operatic and Dramatic Society and had progressed through experience with the D'Oyly Carte Opera Company to becoming one of Novello's favourite leading players in his works.

While Ivor was presenting *The Dancing Years* in Bradford he was also busy writing and planning *Perchance to Dream,* so it is not beyond possibility that his famous song, *We'll Gather Lilacs,* had some of its gestation in an Alhambra dressing room. When *Perchance to Dream* eventually opened in London, Muriel Barron created the parts of Lydia, Veronica and Iris in the three periods of its story.

The famous tenor Richard Tauber was born in Austria, but when in March 1938 the Nazis took possession of Vienna he fled to England where, two years later at the age of forty-seven, he became a naturalised British citizen.

Unfortunately, when he left Vienna there was no time to gather the manuscripts for a musical production he was composing, and they had to be left behind — all except one. That one, however, was to become one of Tauber's most popular and most loved songs, *My Heart and I.* In England Tauber began recreating the score he had been forced to leave in Vienna and when the musical was completed, *My Heart and I* was given pride of place. The show was called *Old Chelsea* and Tauber brought it to the Alhambra in October 1942.

He already knew the theatre for he had previously been to the Alhambra twice with his efforts to off-set the gloom of war. In November 1940 and again in June 1941 he starred in the operetta *Land of Smiles.* It had been written especially for him by the great Franz Lehar, the composer of *The Merry Widow,* still the queen of operettas.

The Land of Smiles contained the song for which Tauber was best known — *You are My Heart's Delight.* He sang it, he calculated, more than 16,000 times. What is certain is that when Tauber's name went up on the billboards the Alhambra became a theatre of smiles.

In 1940 also, an Alhambra bill was headed by the man who had established himself as possibly the most famous ever Danilo in *The Merry Widow.* He was Carl Brisson, who had spent his childhood in a poor quarter of Copenhagen. He started out as a boxer and at the incredibly young age of fifteen won the lightweight championship of Denmark, becoming known as the Danish Carpentier. From being a film actor he went on to the stage as a Variety artist before rising to super-stardom in musical comedy.

He came to Bradford several times and was adored by the lasses of Yorkshire. They were not alone. In London, women, young and old, stood in their hundreds simply to catch a glimpse of him when he left the theatre.

Brisson became very publicity conscious, and in 1932, when he was starring in *The Merry Widow* at the Alhambra, he fooled the Press and pulled off a headline-making ruse. One journalist was later brave enough to confess in print how Brisson had tricked him:

> "The papers on the day it happened had reports of the death of Ivar Kreuger, Sweden's most prominent businessman. He was known as the 'match king' and had been found lying on his bed with a revolver in his hand and a shot through the heart.

> "During an interval in *The Merry Widow* a member of Brisson's staff came to me and said that Kreuger's death had given Carl a great shock, that his association with Kreuger might make a story, but that if I went to the dressing room I would have to be very tactful and after some general conversation refer to Kreuger's death in a casual way.

> "So round to the dressing room I went. Brisson was very charming, offered me a glass of whisky, asked me how I liked the show and then, feeling that this was the right moment, I mentioned Kreuger. What an odd act followed! The smiling Brisson became the tragedian. 'Oh Ivar, Ivar!' he cried.

> "It was only with the utmost difficulty that I could get him to talk, but finally I learned that he and the dead millionaire had been the closest of friends, that they had once had a one-hundred-mile motor race, that Kreuger had tried to get Brisson into Swedish films, knowing that a Brisson film would be popular, and that he had even offered to build Brisson a theatre if he would go to Sweden.

> "But Brisson, by now recovering from the shock, told me that he preferred Britain. I was completely deceived and Brisson got the extra publicity he wanted. Unfortunately Kreuger's suicide was the prelude to a great financial crash in Sweden and when Brisson came to Bradford again I reminded him of his story. With the brightest smile he said: 'Yes, I slipped up there, didn't I?'"

In the Mood with the Stage Bands

"Fans besieged him at the station and throughout the entire evening for his autograph", read a report when Joe Loss and his band played at the Bradford Press Ball in 1937.

No-one was a bit surprised. The age of the British big bands was well established by then and would continue to hold sway throughout the 1940's and, in the case of one or two of the leading ones, well into the fifties.

The band leaders became more than popular figures at big dances, smart-set occasions in the West End and prestige events. Radio made them celebrities in everybody's home and the desire to see them on a stage grew quickly. Variety met that desire and soon, at many theatres, the entire second half of the bill was given over to these new entertainment stars and their musicians.

The Alhambra was no exception. Bradford flocked to see and hear the bands of such orchestral bigs as Roy Fox, Jack Hylton, Harry Roy, Jack Payne, Oscar Rabin and Debroy Somers. Henry Hall was a particular favourite, as were Joe Loss, with his famous *In the Mood* signature tune, and Billy Cotton with his cries of *"Wakey, Wakey!"*

Henry Hall visited Bradford so many times that he became extremely fond of the place. He even broadcast some of his famous guest-nights from the Alhambra, although most people were unaware of it until they switched on their sets to hear that familiar voice say: "This is Henry Hall speaking from the Alhambra, Bradford." Years later Henry said: "The Alhambra is one of the happiest theatres I have ever played in."

I don't know anyone who has met Joe Loss and hasn't liked him. His enthusiasm for life is instantly infectious. Even on his seventy-fifth birthday in June, 1984, he was conducting his fifteen-strong band at London's Berkeley Hotel before setting off on the road again. Joe began broadcasting in 1934 and recalled: "Vera Lynn did her first broadcast with me. I used to pay her about thirty shillings (£1.50) a broadcast. She wasn't a member of the band — I couldn't afford her."

1934 was also the first year that Billy Cotton starred at the Alhambra and twenty-five years later he and his boys were still throwing large balls of cotton wool at the audience during an *I've Got a Lovely Bunch of Coconuts* finale.

Billy, who in his young days was a motor-racing driver, played football as a member for Brentford. The first question he asked when he arrived at the Alhambra in 1947 was, "Is Park Avenue playing at home on Saturday?" He had played on its ground himself.

Although I have no record of his appearing with his Georgians at the Alhambra, trumpeter Nat Gonella has known the Alhambra stage well — as a solo performer and as a member of some of the bands I have mentioned.

Nat also knew the city, for it was in the early 1940's that Private Nat Gonella of the Pioneer Corps slept on a palliasse in Bradford's Belle Vue barracks and drew ten shillings (50p.) a week net instead of up to £150 a week, a personal share in those days when he toured with his band.

Nat, among the best horn players this country has produced, was a member of a boy's band in revue when he first appeared at the Alhambra. The revue was produced by Archie Pitt, who married Gracie Fields. The Gonella trumpet so impressed and delighted the great Louis Armstrong that more than once Satchmo was heard to declare: "Nat's ma boy!"

Yankee-Doodle-Dandies

Apart from many of the greatest British performers who graced the stage of the Alhambra over the years there have been many illustrious visitors from across the Atlantic.

In 1929, for example, the stage and screen actress Tallulah Bankhead, who was reputed to throw a temperament with Olympic-like fervour, came to the theatre in *Her Cardboard Lover,* with a company which included Cedric Bowden, who afterwards became manager of the Grand Theatre, Leeds.

J. B. Priestley once said of Tallulah: "She was a genuine beauty, not a good actress but certainly not a bad one, and she was not a fool, though she often behaved like one." There was no sign of temperament, or foolishness, when she came to the Alhambra, however. And she was even modest enough to suggest that it was the peculiarity of her name, rather than her acting, which brought her fame — although she hated it as a schoolgirl. She explained that Tallulah was an Indian name and also the name of a river and some falls. It meant 'Love Maiden'.

In the 1930's the Alhambra featured another renowned American star, Sophie Tucker — the "first and last of the red hot mommas". Singing her most famous song, she informed the audience: "Some of these days, You're gonna miss me, honey ..." — and they did.

One of the greatest successes at the Alhambra by an American, though, was achieved in April 1949 by Hollywood star singer Allan Jones. He had a glorious voice which was quickly acknowledged by the Alhambra first-nighters who greeted his every song with "salvos of applause", including the one he had made his own, *The Donkey Serenade* from the film *Firefly,* which starred himself and Jeanette MacDonald.

Allan's wife, the glamorous actress Irene Hervey, was with him and they sang a well-received duet. Watching in the wings was their eleven-year-old son, Jack.´

Allan Jones, a mixture of Yorkshire and Welsh stock, was delighted to be in the area because he could boast Tyke grandparents on his mother's side. His fascination with Yorkshire resulted in his making recordings at Bolton Abbey, at Haworth and at a Bradford textile firm, to be broadcast in a popular radio show he and his wife ran in the States.

Among Allan Jones's most successful screen appearances were those in two Marx Brothers films and by coincidence the bill-topper at the Alhambra the following week was Chico Marx.

Son Jack, of course, grew up to be a vocalist almost as famous as his father, and in April 1980 he too stepped on the Alhambra stage and into the Bradford limelight. He once told me, when recalling his earlier visit with his parents: "Believe me, Bradford's a city I shall never forget. I was about ten or eleven and I remember vividly standing in the Alhambra wings doing the off-stage voice for dad's famous *Donkey Serenade* number. But even more vividly I recall the digs where we stayed, together with the comedy duo, Hackford and Doyle, who were on the same bill.

"At those digs it was the first time I had ever seen a chamber pot. It was such a novelty that I decided I just had to try it out. The trouble was that when I woke up next morning I'd forgotten all about it. You don't need three guesses to know what happened next. Yes, I went and put my foot in it. Do I remember Bradford!"

Laurel and Hardy

History will probably look upon the appearances by Laurel and Hardy at the Alhambra in July 1952 and May 1954 as the most prestigious visits ever by American entertainers to that theatre. Yet in those days many Variety enthusiasts didn't see it that way. Laurel and Hardy certainly didn't.

Those who now rush to the television when one of their 300-plus films is shown rightly revere the pair as two of the funniest men this world has known. It could well be in years to come that their names will shine even brighter than those of Keaton, Lloyd and (dare I even suggest it?) Chaplin.

Nevertheless, it wasn't always so. Stan Laurel, from Ulverston, near Barrow, England, and Oliver Hardy, from Georgia in the American South, were so prolific in their output that their films became commonplace on cinema hoardings. So commonplace, indeed, that they were thought ordinary and a bit juvenile". Consequently they were usually screened as second features or "supports".

Happily, most of us now appreciate that there is hardly one movie in that great mass of their work which doesn't bear some mark of comic genius. But most people were still blind to this in the fifties and quite a number of them thought Laurel and Hardy were more suited to a comic strip in the *Film Fun* paper for children than to some future pantheon of immortal drolls. The Alhambra wasn't even crowded for their two visits and many were the passers-by who considered them has-beens;

They themselves were beginning to wonder if they were. They told me that no offer of a film had come their way for a long time — "although we are willing to make a new one if invited."

At the Alhambra they weren't even getting big money. A weekly £250 was shared between them, if the figure whispered in my ear is correct. Many major stars were paid a lot more than that at the time. Yet, as always, Laurel and Hardy slogged their hearts out when they stepped on to the Alhambra stage and performed their hilarious sketches.

Oliver Hardy said of his partner: "To me he is still the finest comedian in the world. I still laugh at him. We have never had a cross word. We have both come up the hard way and there is no jealousy. We can each do things the other can't.

It was through Stan Laurel that Charlie Chaplin got the starring role in one of Fred Karno's most successful sketches, *Jimmy the Fearless, or The Boy 'Ero* in 1910. The part of Jimmy had been originally offered to Chaplin who for some reason turned it down and Karno gave it to a new boy, Stanley Jefferson. After seeing the first performance Chaplin went to Karno and said that he had made a mistake and Jefferson obligingly agreed to back down and take a part in another sketch. Stan Jefferson was, of course, Stan Laurel.

"... after that," he later said. "I used to kid him — always very proudly — that for once in my life Charlie Chaplin was my replacement."

Black is Beautiful

Proportionately, there have not been many Black artists at the Alhambra over the years. But those performing there caused a big impact, all the more memorable because of their small numbers. It's my hope we shall see many more of them in the future. The influence Black people have had, and continue to have, on 20th century music, entertainment and art is colossal. Had it not been for them there would have been neither jazz nor rock music which have given our age two of its more distinctive characteristics. White people are immeasurably in their debt.

As I have referred to ballet it shouldn't be forgotten that there have been some excellent all-Black dance companies at the Alhambra. In memory, pride of place goes to the magnificent-looking company of Zulu tribesmen and women who staged the brilliant *Ipi-Tombi.* "Bradford is fortunate to be able to see a musical which, for sheer excitement of physical power, naked beauty, blood-pounding drumming and swirling colour, makes nearly every other modern show seem as inviting as a wet afternoon in Luddendenfoot." I wrote. I don't take back a word. It was Ipi-Tomfastic!

Of individual Black artists at the Alhambra, perhaps the most striking (as a person as well as an entertainer) was the gentle but tenacious giant of song, Paul Robeson. Before his death, this son of a runaway slave and the holder of a law degree, had been living in seclusion for eleven years in Philadelphia, almost neglected by the America which in 1950 took away his passport for eight years because of his admiration for the Soviet Union and his outspoken championing of American Negro rights.

Paul Robeson died, aged 77, in January 1976 — the same month as did Arnold Ridley, of Dad's Army's Private Godfrey fame, who acted several times at the Alhambra where his play, *The Ghost Train,* was performed more than once.

Years ago, and hours before curtain-up, I met Paul Robeson on a wet October afternoon at the Exchange Station, Bradford. With a pearly smile that shone through the murk and drizzle, he stepped from his train and immediately signed his autograph for two women railway cleaners over whom he towered like a friendly mountain.

Leaving them with grins to match his own, he went straight to his room at the Victoria Hotel where he enthusiastically talked to me about folk music, Yorkshire --- and cricket!

"I think the people of Yorkshire are more distinctive than the people of any other county in England," he said. "This isn't my first time in Bradford and I shall always remember the warm welcomes I have received here."

Of cricket, he remarked: "I like the game immensely. I expect one of the reasons I got interested was through my good friend Leary Constantine who played here, in Bradford, for some time."

Paul Robeson, whose favourite books included J. B. Priestley's *Good Companions,* made a point of answering those who had been criticising his use of the microphone during his recitals. He declared: "I have always used one. Sometimes it may have been hidden, but used correctly it is an asset."

This was an interesting comment, because for a long time the pros and antis argued fiercely about the use of the microphone by stage artists.

I recall, for instance, the late G. H. Elliott (one of the Alhambra's great Variety stars, who even in his later years was as light as a feather as he danced across the stage during his songs) telling me: "A stage is built to move on. But some of the singers today don't seem to need a stage. They might just as well stand on a platform, because they hang on to that microphone as if their lives depend on it — which they probably do!"

Nevertheless, the microphone was here to stay — although it was to have some comic effects sometimes. I couldn't help chuckling, remembering when, in an Alhambra pantomime, singer Ronnie Hilton, unsuccessfully tried to conceal one in the red-spotted handkerchief bundle he carried over his shoulder as Dick Whittington.

"Diddy" David Hamilton, too, who, otherwise was a splendid Buttons in an Alhambra Cinderella panto, had trouble for a short time with a throat mike — although not as much as Ruby Murray did when she played Snow White at the Alhambra. The colleen from Belfast, who once had five hits in the Top 20 (and only Elvis Presley equalled that), was also using a throat mike when the off-stage aerial picked up a local police call. Imagine singing *Someday My Prince Will Come* when seemingly out of your mouth comes the voice of Z for Zebra someone or other calling V for Victor god knows who!

Of Black artists at the Alhambra one male and two women solo pianists were exceptional. For all her "Brr-brr busy lines" and "Chee-Chee" gimmicks, Rose Murphy in the 1950's was a keyboard wonder. She had an exquisitely delicate touch and a lovely sense of rhythm which confirmed that the girl from Cleveland, Ohio, had a very rare talent.

Trinidad-born Winifred Atwell was so popular at the height of her fame, that "house-full" notices had to be put up whenever she appeared. When she pulled-up her chair to her open-fronted "other piano", her diamond bracelet sparkled like a thousand stars as she crashed into the strains of *Britannia Rag* or the *Black and White Rag.* Her brown satin fingers danced over the ivories like dervishes inspired. Yet it was as if she couldn't believe in her own supremacy. "I wish sometimes she would blow her own trumpet more," said her manager adding with a chuckle: "Trumpet, trumpet! Perhaps I could have phrased that better."

The male pianist, who would dab the perspiration from his brow with a white handkerchief after singing, with passionate intensity, such romantic songs as *Begin the Beguine,* was Leslie Hutchinson — or Hutch as he was known. Encouraged by Cole Porter, who brought him to the fore, he was an immaculate and incomparable cabaret master.

Americans, Layton and Johnstone, with their songs at the piano, were adored by packed audiences until they split up in the mid-1930's. Layton, at the keyboard, carried on as a solo act — and with the blessing of all jazz musicians. For it was Turner Layton who composed two of jazz's great standards *Way Down Yonder In New Orleans* and *After You've Gone.* Tragically, Clarence Johnstone slipped into penury when he returned to the States and died penniless in a ramshackle tenement in New York.

Adelaide Hall, who is also revered in jazz because of the classic *Creole Love Call* solo she sang for Duke Ellington in their Cotton Club days, knew Bradford well. She was at the Alhambra with the *Blackbirds* musical in the 1920s, and was there in a *Thanks For the Memory* show as late as the early 70's.

A Black singer who made a big Alhambra impression in 1952 was Billy Banks, an American jazz vocalist who had his first break at Connie's Inn, New York, before having an unbroken residency of 7,151 performances (much of it with Noble Sissle's band) at Billy Rose's Diamond Horseshoe in that same city.

Billy and I were walking down Bradford's Darley Street one day (with every head turning because Billy was the first Black person many of them had seen in a Bradford street) when he showed me the scars on his hands, the outcome of the blisters he had received in the heat of a bottle factory — for he had had a rough and tough struggle in his youth.

Billy, who died in Tokyo in 1967, was a friend of many of the giants of jazz, particularly the greatest of all soprano sax players, Sidney Bechet. He told me this story about the maestro:

"It happened at a country club at St. Louis. There was a golf course adjoining the clubhouse and Sidney would walk out to the links to start his playing every night. When the band struck up *A Pretty Girl Is Like A Melody,* you could hear Sidney playing faintly in the distance through the open doors. It used to delight the crowds.

"On this particular night, however, we could just hear Sidney starting the melody when, between every few notes, he would stop and, in an agitated voice, say, 'Hey, git down there boy! Git down there.' He evidently became more and more alarmed; for suddenly he bounced into the room puffin' and blowin' and pursued by two enormous dogs. I reckon that was the hottest saxophone Sidney ever played. You ought to have heard that crowd roar!"

Final Panto

Francis Laidler's last pantomime, *Red Riding Hood,* opened at the Alhambra on December 27th, 1954. Tragically, he never saw it. His absence at the first night was noticed — he had never been known to miss one — but nobody in the audience was aware that earlier in the day he had suffered a heart attack. Ten days later, on the morning of January 6th, 1955, he died — just one day before his eighty-eighth birthday.

As her husband would have wished, Gwladys Stanley Laidler immediately announced that his pantomimes, *Red Riding Hood* at the Alhambra and *Babes in the Wood* at the Theatre Royal, Leeds, would be unaffected by the 'Governor's' death. "The tradition that the show must go on was sacrosanct to him," she said.

Revered by long-time business rival Emile Littler as "the doyen of theatre managers and a great personal friend", Francis Laidler had lived, slept and dreamed of pantomimes and the stage for the greater part of his life — and often on his own. For Gwladys, a bustling human dynamo, was frequently absent from their suite at the Victoria Hotel. She called herself his "backroom girl" as, basing herself principally at the London flat, she concerned herself with many of the practicalities of their theatrical business as well as contributing to the designs of some of Laidler's productions. Besides, she had a large circle of society and theatre friends in the capital and there was no Caprice or Claridges's in Yorkshire. In ostentatious fur coat and huge picture hat, she was instantly recognisable in the West End, where she could confidently display the whiteness of her gloves. "Oh, they do get so dirty when I'm in Bradford!"

Sincerely Yours

[handwritten signatures including:]

F. Haidler.

Kathleen West.

Walter Niblo

Jory Beattie

Vedmin Dag

Rotherandshire & Aberdonians

Esther Denton

Trevor Myoxelt

Wayne.

Betty

Melanie Paul   Brian Baines

Percy Garside.

FRANCIS LAIDLER'S

Luncheon

to his Artistes of

"CINDERELLA"
PANTOMIME

ALHAMBRA, BRADFORD

22nd December, 1951—15th March, 1952

GT. NORTHERN VICTORIA HOTEL
BRADFORD

MONDAY, 3rd MARCH, 1952

"When Mrs. Laidler was away, you could hardly tell that Mr. Laidler was in the building," was the recollection of a member of the Victoria Hotel staff. "He was as quiet as a mouse. He rarely spoke as he went up to or came down from his suite. He had all his meals served there on his own plates and dishes and with his own cutlery. He insisted on that.

"When he knew that Mrs. Laidler was due to arrive he was a very different man. He would smile and even jest with us and sometimes have a passing word with visitors. He was like a little boy in his excitement."

If evidence were needed that Laidler loved passionately the woman whom he had made a famous principal boy, it was there the day a waiter knocked and walked straight in through the unlocked door of their suite only minutes after Gwladys's arrival. Flushing red, he fled. The couple were in an intimate embrace — to put it euphemistically.

Gwladys loved her husband in return. After his heart attack at the hotel she was at his bedside for forty-eight hours without a break. Being a holiday it had not been possible to engage a nurse and when he was taken to the Duke of York Home, Bradford, she was almost constantly by his side, even when he was periodically given oxygen.

At the Duke of York Home she told reporters that Francis was very ill and added: "But if he comes through this his brain will still go on preparing and presenting pantomimes, even if he is a sick man. He does not like anyone to know he is ill, and when Peter Holdsworth, the journalist telephoned on Monday, despite his heart attack, he took hold of the telephone and said he had only a slight cold like most people at this time of the year."

Francis Laidler's death brought sorrow to countless stage performers. For them, Jack Storey, then starring at the Alhambra, put it well when he said: "I don't think there will ever be another Francis Laidler. He has been wonderful to work for. Working for him was like working for a father. Mr. Laidler had so much sympathy and understanding. Many times you may have thought he was wrong, but in the end he was always right. He was what I call a real producer and he could always get what he wanted without any show of temper or force. I can say without any theatrical hokum that we have all been better for having worked for him."

Francis Laidler, who, after the duty was paid, left more than £50,000, was privately cremated after a funeral service notable for its informal air as well as for its sense of loss.

It took place at Bradford Cathedral, which stands solid and high on Church Bank overlooking the city centre. Even with its elegant extensions by architect Sir Edward Maufe, it still has a no-nonsense exterior as bluff as the old West Riding spirit.

On January 10th, 1955, where pikes had once clashed and muskets roared during the Civil War, large crowds gathered in silence at the gates of the Cathedral. Inside its walls the Archdeacon of Bradford (the Venerable Kenneth Kay) said to the congregation of six hundred: "Thousands of people outside this church today will be remembering with happiness the memory of Francis Laidler. No better tribute could be given to anyone."

There were no distinctions in the placing of the congregation — a fact which would have appealed to Laidler. Stage personalities, some of them with names known in every home in the land, shared pews with the Smiths and Joneses — the ordinary folk who had come to say 'thank you' to one who had given so much pleasure. They heard the Archdeacon say that Francis Laidler had brought a touch of beauty into the lives of many people who otherwise knew nothing other than the drab.

As well as a mayoral party and representatives of many charities, the assembly included the Bishop of Bradford (Dr. A. W. F. Blunt) in his office as president of the Actors' Church Union, such Laidler panto favourites as Albert Modley and Bunny Doyle, and numerous luminaries from theatre managements and staffs.

Among them were Bernard Beard (manager of St. George's Hall, Bradford), Thomas Sunter (manager of the Bradford Prince's), John Beaumont (managing director of the Empire, Leeds), Stanley Joseph (of Leeds City Varieties' Joseph family), Jack Frettingham (manager of the Halifax Palace) and G. W. 'Phil' Ridler (manager of the Bradford Gaumont Cinema), who in earlier days had appeared in shows with Charlie Chaplin. Also there was Fred Hutchins who had been call-boy at the Bradford Empire in 1911.

The Cathedral was heavy with the scent of flowers and among the many perfumed wreaths were those from Wilfred and Mabel Pickles, Norman Evans, Val Parnell and the directors of Moss Empires, George and Alfred Black, Prince Littler, Dorothy Ward and Shaun Glenville, Lawrence Wright and Harry Hanson. But the most touching was the one of red roses from Gwladys Laidler. It was in the shape of a heart.

While the memorial service was taking place a leader writer of the Bradford *Telegraph & Argus* was busy penning the following:

> "Francis Laidler will be remembered for long years to come. Young people who see his pantomime this year, who remember those of last year and the year before will, when they grow old, say, as old people are inclined to say, 'Today's shows are not as good as they used to be', and they will recall Francis Laidler and his achievements.

> "He gave his life to the theatre, and although there is no doubt he had adequate material reward for his labours, he deserves a further tribute for services rendered — a word of gratitude for the pleasure he brought to his fellow men. It would be a poor world without entertainment. To the entertainers, therefore, and to such impresarios as he, without whose organising ability the entertainers could not present their shows, the public is in debt.

> "Mr. Laidler had his critics. There are a number of people who imagined that because the only two live theatres in the city — the Alhambra and the Prince's — were controlled by one man, Bradford did not get as many good shows as it would if there had been a competitor in the field.

> "How little those critics knew of the theatre! How little they realised that had it not been for Mr. Laidler's enterprise and sound management, Bradford might not have been able to boast of two theatres.

> "So far as his own achievements are concerned, this excellent showman was too modest to boost himself personally. It was the theatre, not Francis Laidler, about which he thought.

> "In the same way he did much charitable work, for which he sought no applause. In fact, probably no-one will ever know how great was his contribution to deserving causes.

> "His passing deserves the tribute of a tear."

First Lady of the Alhambra

Bradford City Magistrates granted the formal transfer of the licence of the Alhambra Theatre from the late Francis Laidler to his widow, Gwladys, on January 24th 1955.

It confirmed that she was now the most powerful woman in provincial British theatre. For as well as the Alhambra she controlled her late husband's other theatres — the Bradford Prince's, the Leeds Theatre Royal and the Keighley Hippodrome.

She was fortunate in another way, it transpired, for the secretary based at the Alhambra was the person who had been Laidler's right-hand man for much of the Alhambra's life. As well as having an astute business brain, Rowland Hill had a fine theatrical instinct and a love for the Alhambra which ran unabated. Now Gwladys's loyal adviser and helpmate, Rowland Hill was, in ensuing years, to become second only to Laidler in being a remarkable Alhambra supremo.

Not that Gwladys didn't throw herself with customary zeal into captaining the Alhambra. In spite of the sadness she felt, she whirred with keenness to uphold the Laidler traditions — especially those of pantomimes.

Although she retired as a principal boy in the mid-thirties, Gwladys's stage career was far from over, she thought. "The retirement came," she said, "because Francis had asked me to leave the stage. Our joint earnings were such that tax was an exorbitant drain on us. Come the 1939-45 war, however, I felt, like so many did, that I had to do my bit."

Gwladys Stanley Laidler. "First Lady of The Alhambra." (1938)

She was attached to the War Office and made permanent guest artiste with the *Bombshells* concert party. With it, she entertained thousands of troops, travelling from the Orkneys to the Scilly Isles and Northern Ireland.

Gwladys, who helped direct the shows, said; "We played anywhere — from the largest garrison theatres down to a lonely searchlight site with only a handful of men for an audience ... It was a great experience for me and I swore that if ever I returned to the stage after the war I should never again quibble about the No. 1 dressing-room. With the *Bombshells* I didn't know where I would dress. It might be a perfectly equipped theatre, a barn full of hay or on the draughty deck of a ship. It was all part of the show."

For her work with the *Bombshells,* plus her many efforts to help young people, Gwladys received an MBE in 1946.

Gwladys Laidler made her first broadcast in 1931 and later took part in several of the *Henry Hall's Guest Night* programmes. After one of her broadcasts a critic wrote: "She proved herself an excellent performer for the microphone. Her voice came over sweet and clear. What was more, she introduced novelty into her 'turn'. She pretended to have forgotten her music, but with the aid of her pianist, she built up her next song from stray thoughts, about love in the moonlight and so on. It is to be hoped that she will soon be heard again."

Gwladys wasn't too keen about television, though. Soon after taking over the Alhambra she was interviewed in a Granada magazine programme for women. "I was terrified," she said afterwards. Even so, the Press commented later: "Wearing a fur coat and a large feather hat, Gwladys Stanley Laidler gave a delightful account of her experiences as one of this country's most famous principal boys."

Gwladys was determined to follow in her late husband's footsteps and because of this took on an enormous challenge. For the first time she would be, she decided, a pantomime producer — not of one panto, but two! In addition she would write the scripts and lay down a condition which had never been made before — that the principals should arrive at the first rehearsal word perfect. Those pantomimes were the 1955-56 *Robin Hood* at the Alhambra and *Sleeping Beauty* at the Theatre Royal, Leeds.

Gwladys travelled hundreds of miles as, for weeks, she sped back and forth between Bradford and Leeds to produce her first two pantomimes. *Sleeping Beauty* with Terry Scott and Billy Whittaker, opened on Christmas Eve, 1955, and was an immediate success. "Mrs. Laidler", reported one critic, "reveals remarkable talents, not only as the author of the script, but as a woman sure and certain of production methods ...".

Critical reaction was almost identical when *Robin Hood* opened at the Alhambra on Boxing Day. One reviewer spoke for them all when he wrote: "Gwladys Stanley Laidler has used outstanding ingenuity in the direction of her first Bradford pantomime. She has retained all the essentials of traditional pantomime as envisaged by her late husband, but she has also included a host of original effects and ideas which carried this spectacular show along at a brisk, refreshing pace. The abundance of comedy is one of the most memorable features of her *Robin Hood.*"

Several months before her two pantomimes opened Gwladys called the Press to declare that although she would be introducing changes into the shows, it would be wrong to think that they would represent a break with tradition. Foremost among these changes was "the elimination of horror and poverty". There were to be no impoverished widows hiding from the rent man at the Alhambra or the Leeds Theatre Royal. "Too many people," Gwladys said, "have to eke out an existence without being reminded of it in the theatre. They want to be jolly and cheered up."

She was equally determined "to take the horror out of pantomime". She explained: "The title of *Babes in the Wood* at the Alhambra is to be changed to Robin Hood.

In the show the robbers will be figures of fun entirely. I don't believe in all that business of men taking infants into the wood and threatening them with death. The time is gone when children ought to be frightened in the theatre. After all, the whole thing is a game. Slapstick comedy is coming back into its own. Pantomime is primarily for children and I find that what makes them laugh will amuse the grown-ups too.''

In the 1980's these views may seem ingenuous, but Gwladys believed in them with total sincerity. They belonged to a woman who was a genuinely nice person and wanted the world to be the same, especially if it was the world of the theatre. It's not a bad way to be remembered.

Scene 3	... ...	NAUTICAL NONSENSE
The Dancers ... Vadier & Dorinova	And Our Lovely Laughing Ladies	
Scene 4	... ...	" WASHING DAY " (Dan Leno, Jr.)
Mrs. West .... NELLIE WALLACE		
Her Husband ...... Neville Delmar	Mrs. Thomas .... Billy Bernhart	
Scene 5	... ...	" THE PICTURE HAT "
The Boy .... Lewis Barber	The Girl .... Maudie Francis	
And Our Beautiful Blondes		
Scene 6	... ...	" MEET ME VICTORIA " (Lauri Wylie)
The first Passer-by . Ralph Humble	The Romantic Man . Neville Delmar	
The other Passer-by . Fred Gratton	The Romantic Lady	
	NELLIE WALLACE	

Page from a 1935 programme

Unpredictable City

Hardly had Mrs. Laidler's first two pantomimes ended before she displayed quite out-of-character irritation because of the lack of public support for some of the other attractions she had brought to the Alhambra.

She had failed to appreciate that she was in no different a position than many other theatre owners. The trouble was that by the mid-fifties Variety was drying up. Old stalwarts like Wilson, Keppel and Betty and 'Wee' Georgie Wood, and not so old ones like Ted Lune and Johnny Lockwood, did their utmost to keep it going, but it was a fight against the inevitable, and many artists knew it.

In his Alhambra dressing room comedian Terry Thomas dropped his "Good Lawrd, old boy" image to inform me: "Variety is in the doldrums. Television is changing people's habits more subtley and perniciously than any of us imagined. Even the public houses are doing poor business. But the off-licence shops are doing fine. Why? Because many people are taking a bottle home to drink while watching TV."

A few weeks earlier in that same dressing-room, Vic Oliver (The Old Vic, as he was nicknamed) was in a similar downcast mood. "I know that Variety is in a mess and that television is taking over," he said. "But I refuse to appear on it, as a comedian anyway. A comic who discloses all his patter before an audience of millions is cutting his own throat. He can't tour with it after that!"

Vic's words were prophetic. Many comics did fade all too quickly after using up their material in no time at all on the small screen. Vic Oliver stuck to his guns, but others like him rapidly became fewer and fewer.

Variety theatres had therefore to look to plays for replacements, plus the few big attractions of major touring companies, but they were getting less in number too. Even though permanent repertory companies had been at the Prince's Theatre for years, Bradford had never had a large playgoing populace and consequently, unless there was a performer with huge mass appeal, or a television star in a play at the Alhambra, the theatre rarely did well at the box-office.

When the Alhambra opened in 1914 there were more than 1,000 theatres operating in Britain, but by the early 1980's the number of those still in use for their original purpose had dwindled alarmingly.

In March, 1956, of course, Gwladys Laidler was not able to foresee this when she let fly at Bradford audiences for being "absolutely unpredictable". In Bradford, it appeared, even a famous ex-ballerina was not a guarantee of success.

"I was determined to try to bring good shows to the Alhambra from the start," she insisted. "But if people here were really interested in the arts as they were said to be, they would have flocked, for instance, to see an unusual play like *I am a Camera* which starred Moira Shearer. Instead the week's business at the Alhambra was worse than that in any other city in the country.

"I find it impossible to tell what Bradford audiences want ... I brought *Airs on a Shoestring,* the London smash-hit revue, straight from the capital after a two-year run, but people didn't turn up to see it.

"I must emphasise, however," she added, "that I cannot grumble about pantomime audiences. They have responded excellently."

In acknowledging the importance of pantomime, though, Gwladys Laidler had put her finger on the Alhambra's saving grace. Without the income from its pantomimes the Alhambra could not survive and that was to apply right up to the final 1983-84 panto at the "old" Alhambra, when The Krankies, Billy Dainty and Peter Goodwright starred in *Babes in the Wood.*

The "old" Alhambra was essentially a theatre for Bradford. The hugely improved "new" Alhambra is a regional one, serving a catchment area of six million people. Great spectacular shows should prove to be its by right, but, as Gwladys Laidler found out, the Alhambra almost certainly will still need its annual pantomime.

Queen of Pantomime and Queen of his Heart

In September 1956 Gwladys was in a London nursing home recovering from an operation. "I am making a speedy recovery," she reported in a letter, "and working myself into a positive frenzy about my two forthcoming pantomimes, *Sleeping Beauty* in Bradford and *The Queen of Hearts* at the Theatre Royal, Leeds. (She did not know it, but the latter was to change her life.)

"I am really looking forward to being in Yorkshire again," she continued, "despite the fact that I shall leave here sans gall bladder, sans appendix — and sans the Hippodrome, Keighley."

Her reference to the Keighley theatre was written confirmation that the Laidler enterprises were not succeeding as well as she had anticipated. Business at the Hippodrome had become desperate, so it had to go. Sold for conversion into business premises, it was pulled down five years later, in 1961, to make way for a bus station.

Nevertheless, in the minds of most stage people, Gwladys Stanley Laidler was still a remarkable woman — and still the Queen of Pantomime. She had been given this regal title on the last night of her *Sleeping Beauty* at the Theatre Royal, Leeds, when Billy Whittaker, the Dame, brought on to the stage a throne-like chair as Gwladys was thanking the players for their performances Billy interposed, asked Gwladys to sit down and, addressing the audience, said: "Mrs. Laidler's late husband, Mr. Francis Laidler, was known for many years as the King of Pantomime. Now in her own right Gwladys Stanley Laidler has proved herself the veritable Queen." With that, and to resounding applause, Billy placed a silver crown on Gwladys's head.

As soon as Gwladys was out of hospital she threw herself into the preparations for her two pantomimes at the Alhambra and the Theatre Royal, Leeds. However, in late November, a month before *The Queen of Hearts* was to open, she announced that she would be selling the Theatre Royal.

"I have no option but to sell the place," she said. "Death duties and that shocking entertainment tax have forced me to it. I do not know whether I shall be able to face the Theatre Royal panto's last night this time. It will be a moment of grief, for my personal success and my marital happiness were bound up in that theatre."

But Gwladys *was* there at the Theatre Royal in March 1957 on the final evening of *The Queen of Hearts*. It was just as well she was, for she was introduced to the man who was, in four month's time, to become her new husband. He was Mr. Frank Woodhead, a widower and chairman of Toledo Woodhead Springs Ltd., of Sheffield and Aycliffe, a company he had founded twenty years previously. The couple became engaged on June 28th, 1957 and were married at Caxton Hall, London, in July.

Alhambra on Offer

Immediately after *The Queen of Hearts* panto the eighty-year-old Theatre Royal shut its doors permanently to make way for a department store, but even before this it had become obvious that the Alhambra and Prince's theatres were also threatened.

The Alhambra Theatre, May 1958
(Note the 'Chocolate Domes', a leftover from wartime camouflage)

On December 20th, 1956, the local Valuation Court in Bradford heard that receipts at the Alhambra had fallen in the past three years by £10,000, and in the past five years by £20,000. The receipts at the Prince's in the past year had been £18,000 down on the figure for 1945.

Because of this the court reduced the rateable value of the Alhambra from £1,913 (gross £2,300) to £1,555 (gross £1,870) and of the Prince's from £872 (gross £1,050) to £780 (gross £940).

But it wasn't enough. Like scores of other privately operated theatres, the Alhambra and the Prince's were fighting a losing box-office battle.

In 1982 the Recreation Divison of Bradford Metropolitan Council published an interesting and all-important study. It was called *The Alhambra Theatre — To Be or Not To Be, That Is The Qestion*. Considering the number of people who were going to play Hamlet about the public money which eventually was spent on the Alhambra, it was perhaps an ironic title.

Perceptively, the study pinpointed the causes of the difficulties encountered by theatres in the mid-fifties. It stated: "Between the wars all theatres enjoyed a run of some years with little opposition from other forms of entertainment; and the immediate post-war years too saw theatre managements having little difficulty in 'getting bums on seats'. Since then, however, the leisure activities of the masses have undergone a dramatic change, brought about by a real increase in personal income resulting in increased ownership of motor cars and the omnipresence of the television set. The greatest changes in leisure activities have occurred where there is a link between the activity and the car or TV. The theatre has, therefore, for some years been in competition with a whole range of leisure activities made accessible to people through the increased mobility provided by the motor car and with the easily obtainable passive entertainment of a generally high quality available on television."

Gwladys Laidler was only too aware of all this when, on June 21st, 1957, — just before her engagement to Frank Woodhead — she offered the Alhambra building to Bradford Corporation at a price of £85,000. Her aim, she explained, was that it should continue as a theatre, and to further this she had been in touch with the Arts Council. She believed that particular body was interested in the idea of developing the theatre under its direction.

Gwladys made no secret of her wish to reduce her theatrical activities, but she added in her written offer: "I am desirous that the Alhambra should remain a theatre, and especially a civic theatre. That would have been the wish of my late husband, Francis Laidler.

"I do feel that the suggestion will meet with the general approbation of all those who have at heart this music-loving theatre of ours; and, in addition the step proposed would protect the amateur productions which have been at the Alhambra for so many years — in fact, the scope in this direction could be enlarged."

On the 23rd July Bradford City Council, which by then had learned that it would not receive any help from the Arts Council if it bought the theatre, decided not to accept the offer. The ball was firmly back in Gwladys's court, but she battled on — supported, of course, by the loyalty and theatrical wisdom of the Alhambra's secretary, Rowland Hill.

Six months later, she was still so vital that she not only produced the 1957-58 *Puss in Boots* at the Alhambra, but she directed a second pantomime at Sheffield where her husband had major business interests.

Nevertheless, on February 17th, 1958, during the run of *Puss in Boots,* Gwladys put the Alhambra up for sale on the open market. Considering the state of the theatre generally it is not surprising that no-one rushed to buy.

A year later, when the 1958-59 pantomime *Dick Whittington* opened, the Alhambra was still on the market, and this time Gwladys was not the producer. The show was a Sam H. Newsome production which, with different stars, had been at the London Palladium the previous year and, before that, at Newsome's own Coventry Theatre.

Dick Whittington was a significant show, for it was the first non-Laidler pantomime in Bradford for well over half a century.

In December 1963 Gwladys Laidler Woodhead became a widow for the second time and shortly afterwards decided that the time had come to end her association with the Alhambra. It was the only Laidler theatre remaining, for the Prince's, bought for demolition by the Council, had finally closed in May 1961.

On September 15th, 1964, a meeting of the nine principal shareholders was held at the Alhambra when 80 per cent of the shareholders agreed that the Bradford Alhambra Theatre Company Ltd. should go into voluntary liquidation. Gwladys, the company's chairman and principal shareholder, signed the last formal documents and it was over: the Bradford-Laidler connection, which had been a major theatrical force for more than sixty years, was ended.

Nevertheless, it was announced that the show would still go on. Bradford City Council finally came up trumps and agreed to buy the Alhambra for £78,900 and leasing it to the newly formed Bradford Alhambra Ltd., under the managing directorship of Rowland Hill. Rent to be paid by the new company was £1,500 a year, plus a third of net profits.

Ten years later, in the summer of 1974, Gwladys Laidler Woodhead died in a hospital in Monte Carlo at the age of seventy-eight. She had spent much of the intervening years in London and in Italy where she had bought a house. She also made a number of trips to America. She was cremated in Marseilles — a long way from the Bradford Alhambra and the sleepy hollow in Staffordshire where she had been brought up.

Gwladys, who left £114,335 gross, was remembered at a special service in London. From the pulpit of the parish church of St. Marylebone, Wilfred Pickles, himself an Alhambra pantomime star, mourned her as "perhaps the most famous principal boy of English pantomime".

Wilfred, recalling how he and his wife Mabel had known Gwladys for fifty years, said: "I admired her as an artist and adored her as a principal boy. To my wife and myself she was one of the greatest friends we ever had. It was happiness and laughter I associated her with. She would often have even younger people falling about laughing as she told stories, often against herself".

There were many who thought likewise about the Gwladys with a 'W', whose last words to me, I remember, were: "Tell Bradford not to let the Alhambra go".

Plumpshus, Tattiphilarious and Discomknockerating

Before the Laidler connection was severed at the Alhambra, there were two of the most exceptional and memorable pantomimes in the theatre's history. But for very different reasons. The first was the 1959-60 *Jack and the Beanstalk* which turned an up-and-coming young Liverpool comic into a star; and the other was the 1961-62 *Puss in Boots* which had to be taken off a month before its scheduled finish.

The day after *Jack and the Beanstalk* opened, I wrote in a review: "If you enjoy laughing then go to see a great comedian. For Ken Dodd is just that. As a Prince of Mirth he's dynamic. He has 'crossed the border' to appear in a Bradford pantomime and for once Yorkshire folk can be jealous of their neighbouring county. Who wouldn't want to own such an incomparable jester? His timing is superb, his delivery is delicious — and what a worker! He is indefatigable. With his wide-eyed vitality, with his irresistible grin beneath a mountainous shock of hair, Ken Dodd, who plays Simple Simon, is the most brilliant artist seen in a Bradford pantomime within my memory. If he can maintain such comical sparkle, he will establish himself among the immortals of Variety.''

There are not many now who wouldn't agree that since that pantomime the Nut from Knotty Ash, Liverpool, has become one of the all-time great theatre comedians. I say theatre comedian because Ken, even with his tickling-stick, which is a derivative of the bladder-on-a-stick of the medieval jesters, needs the challenge of a live audience, not the disciplined artificialities of a TV studio.

Ken Dodd never forgot his success in *Jack and The Beanstalk,* and for a number of years the Alhambra was almost a second home to him. He loved the place and campaigned for its saving and improving. He also, I remember loved fish-and-chip suppers at a nearby shop-cum-eating-place. At one of those meals, when that most jovial of pianists, Mrs. Mills, was one of his guests, a group of young men, who were appearing way down the bill, were in a far corner, tucking in with the fervour of the famished. Ken nudged me. ''Watch out for that lot. They'll go to the top,'' he said. He was right. They were The Grumbleweeds.

As it turned out, Ken was also to be associated with the *Puss In Boots* panto; but in a very different way.

The biggest box-office blow in Alhambra history fell in early February, 1962, when *Puss in Boots* had to close because of the scare following the Bradford smallpox outbreak. Such a shut-down had never been known before.

Thousands of seats had been cancelled by people worried about coming into the city centre. They included coach parties who left huge blocks of seats empty. Tens of thousands of pounds were lost.

Announcing the closure, Mr. Rowland Hill, the director and secretary of the Alhambra, said: ''People have simply been afraid to come into the theatre. We really regret having to take action, but because of the present conditions we find we have no alternative open to us if we are to avoid further losses.''

Puss in Boots, which starred among others George Bolton, a veteran stand-up comic but still one of Variety's best, had looked to have a jinx on it from the start. That brilliant man-mountain in a fez, the late Tommy Cooper, its main star, slipped a disc and had to work in a plaster cast. He was in agony, but patrons never guessed it. His huge grin and his deliberately bungling fun were as zany as ever.

More clouds gathered over the show when principal boy Joy Turpin was unable to wear high heels because of a strapped-up ankle following a slip on some stairs. Then one of the acrobats was admitted to hospital with a tendon injury. Later, many of the cast caught 'flu.

One person, however, was far from scared off by the smallpox crisis. He was Peter Haddon who, much concerned, insisted on filling at least one of the now vacant weeks at the Alhambra with his production of the comedy-thriller *Ghost Squad*. Peter Haddon had an excellent ''rep'' company at Wimbledon; and the previous season he had brought it for a season to the Alhambra. He had been warmly received, and Peter hadn't forgotten that. Among Peter's players was a young and promising Canadian called Al Waxman; and we became friends. Al was to become the detective boss of television's *Cagney and Lacey*.

To coincide with the *Puss In Boots* panto, a big Panto-Press ball was planned to take place at the Mecca, Bradford, the profits from which were to be divided between journalists' charities and the Water Rats (a famous money-raising showbiz fraternity). But by the time of the ball, the panto had closed and its stars had left the city. The organisers of the ball, however, wrote to the stars of other northern pantos, asking them to come along and support what, after all, was half their event. Some of the resultant excuses for not attending hardly needed, I'm sorry to say, to be read to be disbelieved.

In desperation I contacted Ken Dodd who was starring in a big Christmas season show in Manchester. Although he was not then a Water Rat, he didn't hesitate. Not only would he be delighted to come to what most outsiders considered a "plague city", but he arrived at and returned to the ball by taxi and got up on stage and gave close to an hour's spontaneous entertainment which had the dancers a-roar.

Afterwards, Ken refused to accept a penny even towards the cost of his transport. So much for that on stage ribbing by other comics that the King of the Diddymen was "a bit close".

The Man of Devotion

In the programme for the Alhambra gala concert in honour of Rowland Hill on his retirement, Beryl Grey, the former ballerina, wrote: "It was during the last world war that I first met the remarkable Rowland Hill when I came to the Alhambra Theatre at the age of fourteen. I was then dancing with the Sadler's Wells Ballet and I returned annually with them for many years to dance in his theatre. Latterly, since taking over the direction of London Festival Ballet, I have worked more closely with him and come to know and appreciate him even more. He is one of the all-time 'greats' of the theatre. He is a friend of all; a father-figure; someone you can rely upon under any circumstances. His knowledge of the theatre and instinctive feeling for every situation is something that he must surely have been born with and which all his years of devotion in the theatre have strengthened. All of us in the theatre who have worked with him keep a very special place for him in our hearts. I, for one, am inspired by his courage and leadership."

You can't earn a much better appreciation than that and without a man of such strength of character at the helm, the Alhambra would never have survived the tempestuous financial sea Rowland Hill had to navigate between his taking over the theatre in 1964 and his retirement ten years later. Had he failed, the Alhambra might well have become another Morley Street waste.

Rowland Hill was associated with the Alhambra right from the beginning. On that very first night in March 1914 he was there in his brand new chocolate, scarlet and gold page-boy's uniform looking not unlike a miniature Buttons. He was then a fourteen-year-old schoolboy and worked at the Alhambra every evening from when the theatre opened until 9.30 p.m., when he went home to do his homework.

When he left school the following Christmas Francis Laidler gave him a full-time job in the theatre's office and he remained there until 1916 when, because of a minor dispute with a member of the management (not Laidler), his parents advised him to leave. After a spell in the offices of Hey's Brewery and Thomas Cooks he joined the army in November 1917 and remained in service until 1922.

On returning to Bradford he again found a job as an assistant to the Alhambra's company secretary and thus began fifty-two years of uninterrupted association with the theatre — a half-century during which he became Francis Laidler's right-hand man and ultimately himself the boss of the theatre he was to pilot through some of its most difficult days.

When he first joined the Alhambra full-time in 1922 he spent six years of what free time he had in studying accountancy. As a result, in 1928, he became a certified accountant and, seven years later, a member of the Chartered Institute of Secretaries.

Among other important dates were 1937 when he became the Alhambra's assistant secretary, 1938 when he was appointed Laidler's co-director, plus being made secretary of the Alhambra and Laidler's other Yorkshire theatres, and administrator of the Laidler shows. In 1964, of course, he became managing director of the new Alhambra Theatre Company Ltd.

Rowland Hill; Secretary and Director of the Alhambra Theatre, Bradford. May 1986.

During his career Rowland Hill personally managed at various times all of Laidler's theatres as well as administering the Laidler pantomimes. These included the four at the London Coliseum, two at the Victoria Palace and one at Daly's Theatre and the famous one at the Royal Opera House, Covent Garden.

Among Rowland Hill's most vivid memories are those of Francis Laidler. "He was a father-figure and a great gentleman of the theatre," he said. "He could be a bit of a martinet, but I had nothing but kindness from him. With him you never had to procrastinate or make excuses and he was tremendously fair.

"For instance, when his *Mother Goose* was staged at Daly's (it was the last live show there before it was pulled down and the Warner Cinema built on its site), London was hit by a 'flu epidemic and people were begged to keep out of theatres. As a result the show lost £10,000, but Mr. Laidler would not hear of this being met by shareholders. He had presented the show, so, he insisted, he would stand the loss out of his own holding.

"Francis Laidler was always willing to listen and I could not possibly count the number of times in the old days when I walked up the staircase at the Victoria Hotel to Mr. Laidler's suite to discuss business problems with him. I used to go across most nights at about 10 p.m. for meetings with him."

Rowland Hill was to get to know well hundreds of performers. Among them at the Alhambra in the early days were Mark Sheridan, Marie Studholme, Violet Vanbrugh, Weedon Grossmith, Sir Harry Lauder, Eugene Stratton and Albert Whelan, who was the first Variety artist to have a signature tune.

Rowland Hill could just recall seeing as a boy Sara Bernhardt and he named among those he found most delightful Florrie Forde, Charlie Kunz, Ben Lyon and Bebe Daniels, Robb Wilton, Ella Shields, Vic Oliver, Layton and Johnstone, Jimmy Jewel and Ben Warriss, Georgie Wood, Ivor Novello, Dame Sybil Thorndike, Henry Hall, Val Doonican and Norman Evans "who stood out a mile among all Mr. Laidler's pantomimes."

Rowland Hill retired on June 1st, 1974, saying: "I will at least have more time to devote to my two daughters, six grandchildren and, above all, my wife who has had to put up with my long working hours all these years and who has been a brick."

For half-a-dozen years after becoming the boss of the Alhambra Rowland Hill was able to keep content his landlord, the Bradford City Council, which had laid down it should receive a third of the net profit annually as well as the £1,500 annual rent.

Over a period of six years, to 1970, the Council received a share of profits totalling £8,782. However, the Council had also agreed to underwrite any losses and in 1971 it became obvious that a loss would in fact be incurred by the theatre company. This resulted in the City Treasurer presenting a report to the Council's management committee in July 1971 entitled *Theatre in Bradford*.

The City Treasurer stated that the future of theatre in Bradford needed resolving with some urgency and also that if the City Council wished to retain professional live theatre as an amenity and attraction of the city, not only for its residents but also as part of the facilities by which it was hoped new industry and development would be drawn to Bradford, then it was going to have to pay for it.

He also said that if the Council decided to take responsibility for the Alhambra, then it would run the theatre itself rather than through a trust and so retain direct control over the amount of resources to be devoted to this purpose and the broad policy to be followed by the theatre.

In 1974 Bradford Alhambra Ltd. was finally wound up and the management of the theatre was taken over by its then owner, Bradford Metropolitan Council.

Considering the state of the theatre nationally, the ability of Rowland Hill (who recruited Herbert Shutt, of the Ideal Ballroom, as a director) to make a profit at all during those first six years can be now seen not only as a staggering achievement, but as a vital one. For had he "gone under" in the mid-sixties it is almost certain the Alhambra would not have been saved. The time would not then have been ripe for the Council to consider turning 'impresario'.

In 1969, when Rowland Hill was four years past the normal retiring age, he courageously renewed the Alhambra lease. "I was sufficiently proud to think I would be able to make my way unaided," he said later. But two years after that renewal he had to acknowledge: "As things are today a theatre like the Alhambra is no longer a viable proposition."

Robinson Crusoe, 1970-71 Pantomime,
with Tommy Trinder, Jack Tripp, Marion Grimaldi, Allen Christie and the Cox and Miles Twins.

The real trouble, he revealed, was that it had become extremely difficult to book big attractions and that those shows which were willing to tour demanded higher and higher guaranteed fees.

We now know that several major touring companies by-passed the Alhambra because they considered its stage facilities no longer adequate. In other words the "old" Alhambra had almost had its day and this seemed to be also the opinion of the public.

One of the most cherished memories of Rowland Hill's career was the visit by the Bolshoi and Kirov Ballets — not simply because they made a profit of £500, but also because of the fantastic final night when the flower-throwing audience applauded through twenty minutes of curtain calls.

But even that modest profit didn't seem much when compared with the losses of £1,500, £2,000 and £3,000 sustained by other illustrious companies from abroad, including the superb Georgian State Dancers.

On the other hand, there were several happy highlights during the Rowland Hill era, including a Gala production in June, 1969, in aid of the York Minster Appeal, which was attended by the Duke of Edinburgh. There was another Royal visit in June, 1977, when the Princess Anne attended a Gala performance in aid of the Queen's Silver Jubilee Appeal. Among the celebrities in the presentation line-up were Harry Worth, the Beverley Sisters and the diminutive Arthur Askey who, when he noticed that he was standing next to former champion boxer Henry Cooper, commented: "I'll never last a round against him".

Among the most notable productions to be seen at the Alhambra during the Rowland Hill era were the Royal Shakespeare Company's *A Midsummer Night's Dream,* directed by Peter Hall and Peter Brook's highly acclaimed production of Durrenmatt's *The Physicists,* in which Irene Worth, Cyril Cusack, Tony Church and Alan Webb excelled.

From the Bristol Old Vic Company came Stuart Burge's cracking production of Shakespeare's *Henry V* in which Richard Pascoe as Harry of England was "a thunderbolt of valour"; and his wife Barbara Leigh-Hunt appeared in the title role of Bernard Shaw's *Saint Joan* in an impressive production by Christopher Denys. Bernard Shaw wrote *Saint Joan* for Sybil Thorndike and she had a great success in the role at the Alhambra soon after her London triumph.

Perhaps *the* most outstanding event of that time was the marathon four-hour long Val May production of Eugene O'Neills *Mourning Becomes Electra.* It was the first time this trilogy had been presented in Britain for nearly a quarter of a century. In spite of impressive performances by Michael Goodlife and William Sylvester in this London Old Vic production, the night belonged to Barbara Jefford as Lavinia and Sonia Dresdel as her mother, Christine.

A number of plays by the new wave of writers in the late fifties and early sixties were seen at the Alhambra, including Arnold Wesker's *Chips With Everything,* Brendan Behan's *The Hostage,* Alun Owen's *No Trams to Lime Street* and Doris Lessing's *Play With A Tiger* (with the great Siobhan McKenna) which had its premiere in Bradford before going on to win critical acclaim in the West End.

Although musical productions were diminishing, there were still a few which brought in large audiences, especially the *Black and White Minstrels* whose company included the much applauded Leslie Crowther. Vanessa Lee and Peter Graves were in great melodic form in *The Merry Widow* and there were plenty of tuneful items from the *Fol-de-Rols* and from the visiting summer shows from Morecambe presented by Hedley Claxton who was to produce at least one Alhambra pantomime.

The Bernard Miles-Laurie Johnson-Lionel Bart romp *Lock Up Your Daughters* was memorable for the fine performance of Arthur Lowe as the lecherous Justice Squeezum.

Arthur, of course, was famous for his television roles in *Coronation Street* and *Dad's Army* — a stage version of which was later to come to the Alhambra — and he was one of several television stars to appear in straight plays at the Alhambra. Among them were Pat Phoenix, who gave an impressive performance in *The Miracle Worker* as the determined teacher who brought light into the life of the blind, deaf and dumb child, Helen Keller. Pat (under the name Pat Pilkington) was a former repertory actress at the Bradford Prince's.

In its struggle for survival, Variety still managed to provide a few starry memories. An up-and-coming Shirley Bassey, for instance, stunned a twice-nightly audience at the Alhambra with her brilliance. Some years later Rowland Hill invited her back, but her fee had risen so much that he couldn't afford it. Not only was he disappointed, but so was Shirley Bassey who wrote to him privately sending deep regrets. It was the old, old story and one which was eventually to hit the club circuits — agents fix appearance fees, not performers.

Among those (and there were many more) who helped the Alhambra through difficult days, and in no particular order, were Hylda Baker, Julie Andrews, Bill Maynard, Eunice Gayson, Barbara Kelly, Ronnie Corbett, David Nixon, Bruce Trent, Brian Rix, Reg Varney, Norman Vaughan, Max Wall, Al Read, David Whitfield, Barry Sinclair, Richard Todd, Jimmy James, Stephen Murray, Julia Foster, Jean Kent, Richard Murdoch, Dave King, Spike Milligan, Kenny Baker, Nina and Frederick, Cavan O'Connor, Michael Denison, Dulcey Gray, Eddie Calvert, Diana Dors, Valentine Dyall, Thora Hird, Englebert Humperdinck (then called Gerry Dorsey), Jeremy Hawk, McDonald Hobley, Freddie and the Dreamers, Bruce Forsyth, Dick Emery, Douglas Byng, Billy Milton, Freddie Frinton, Jimmy Clitheroe, Jess Conrad and the American singer, Dick Haymes.

Newcomers and Novices

The Alhambra has helped a number of newcomers and "novices" on the way to stardom. It was in *Billy Liar* on August 27th 1962, for example, that Lynn Redgrave, daughter of Sir Michael and sister of Vanessa, made her professional debut on any stage. With a cast that included Trevor Bannister, Frank Pettit and Eileen Dale, she was praised for giving "a splendid piece of acting as the orange-loving, prissy-miss of a girl friend."

Other memorable early appearances won commendation in April 1965 when the National Youth Theatre, under its splendid director Michael Croft, brought Paul Hill's lovely production of *A Midsummer Night's Dream* to the Alhambra. Among the young cast were Helen Mirren and Diana Quick.

Perhaps the most fascinating Alhambra "newcomers" story goes back to the late fifties when Peter Dews, a former Bradford Playhouse producer who achieved fame with his *Age of Kings* on television and then won honours as a distinguished international drama director, showed me a half-finished script of a play called *The Discipline of War*. "I think it's rather good," he said, "but I'm having difficulty in hurrying up the author to finish it." Happily, that script was completed. Its title was changed to *The Long and the Short and the Tall* and it came to the Alhambra.

Some months previously George Devine, the distinguished director of the English Stage Company at London's Royal Court Theatre, had told me that all aspiring playwrights would do well to model themselves on the author of *The Long and the Short and the Tall* — the prolific Willis Hall.

Willis, of course, was to become one of the most gifted writers of his day — including his partnership with Keith Waterhouse which is legendary. It is an accolade for West Yorkshire that he made his home in the Brontë country near Keighley.

Waterhouse and Hall were the authors of the satirical revue, *England Our England* which was presented at the Alhambra in March 1962. Directed by John Dexter, it proved a little too advanced for the liking of many people — which was a shame because it had a cast which now reads like a roll of honour. Among the performers were Dudley Moore, Roy Kinnear, Alison Leggat, Murray Melvin, Barrie Ingham (from Halifax) and brilliant Billie Whitelaw who was brought up in Bradford and still regards it as her home town. She helped with the campaign to save the Alhambra.

Roy Kinnear had appeared in *The Long and the Short and the Tall* when it came to the Alhambra, as had Ilkley's John Colin as the sergeant. The programme itself must now be a collector's item, for cast as the Cockney soldier, Bamforth, was a young actor called Michael Caine.

Five or six years later, when Michael Caine was on the brink of international stardom, he told me: "It was my first significant break when I was chosen for the role of Bamforth. I remember that visit to Bradford well. We had a very happy time there and we were well received. It was quite a remarkable company for a provincial tour. I remember the cast included Terence Stamp and Joseph Brady, as well as Roy Kinnear and John Colin."

The Amateur Companies

"When the amateurs take over it's like the old days," said Rowland Hill when non-professional companies were flourishing. He wasn't so much talking about the standard of their presentation as about the way those companies could attract large audiences — and they weren't all relatives and friends by any means.

In the old days, the girls in amateur operatic societies had to do little more than stand there and look pretty. From the 1950's onwards, however, they were expected to be much more energetic like this line up from a 1974 Alhambra amateur production of Cole Porter's Can-Can.

The contribution of Bradford's major operatic companies to the Alhambra's well-being has been considerable. In fact there were periods during the later years of the "old" theatre when it was doubtful whether the Alhambra would have survived without the business they brought it.

They were not entirely without faults, of course. For instance, until the 1960's when class structures began to crumble, some members of the leading societies gave themselves a social status that their efforts didn't always justify. With some of them too there was an insularity which blocked them from attending many a professional show which desperately needed support.

Nevertheless — and it is a big nevertheless — the virtues of the amateurs who performed at the "old" Alhambra far outweighed their failings. They battled on, for example, when the chances of their shows breaking even, let alone making a profit, became less and less. And they permitted the Bradford area to see many a big-scale musical which, without their efforts, would never have graced the Alhambra stage. In addition, they had an enthusiasm for work and, within their own ranks, a robust camaraderie which were exemplary.

Bradford's amateur dramatics tradition goes back a long way. If you go through the pages of *The Era* — a once famous, if exclusive, theatrical journal — you will find that Bradford had a prosperous amateur theatre company more than a century ago. It was mentioned in *The Era* in 1868 — even if it was perhaps because a certain Jack Nunn, a notable Bradford sportsman, was a member of the company concerned and *The Era's* Bradford correspondent.

Later in the 1880's and the Naughty Nineties, there was the Bradford Amateur Thespian Society, known as *The BATS*. It had such redoubtable players as S. Henry Longbottom, Jerrold Robertshaw, who became a West End actor-manager, and Charles Vernon France who, at the time of his death, was described as "the finest character actor of his day". His biographical details filled four columns in *Who's Who in the Theatre*.

During the same period as The BATS, the Bradford Operatic Society was formed and in December 1890 it took the Prince's Theatre for a week and presented two grand operas — *The Bohemian Girl* and *Maritana*. In one of them was John Coates who only a few years later was acclaimed as one of England's finest tenors. This opera company was formed by pupils of Madam Ter Meer, an outstanding teacher and violinist.

At the dawn of the twentieth century local musical stage enthusiasts were pressing to extend their activities. Consequently, in 1903, what was to become the city's longest established company of its kind was launched — Bradford Amateur Operatic and Dramatic Society, several of whose original members were also pupils of Madam Ter Meer. Although dormant of late it had, apart from the war years, a busy history until a few years ago.

For more than half a century the Bradford Amateurs, as the Bradford AO and DS is commonly known, enriched the Alhambra's calendar, to be followed by the Bradford Players (formed in 1926 and with their early shows at the Prince's Theatre).

It was the Bradford Players company which had to confront a most unusual problem. Because of a fire in 1936 at the electricity works, Bradford's power supply failed. In spite of efforts to light the stage by driving a car up the theatre's scenery ramp and shining headlights down on to the stage, there wasn't enough illumination and the performance of *The New Moon* was cancelled.

From the early 1950's there came the Bradford Gilbert and Sullivan Society (specialists of the Savoy Operas) who adopted their constitution in 1949. Later to the Alhambra stage came the Bradford Catholic Players, formed in 1927 as the St. Joseph Players who presented their early productions at the Parish Hall in Clayton Lane; The Great Horton Amateurs, who started as a glee union in 1904 in a school hall and who by

1939 had expanded so much that they presented *Rose Marie* at the Alhambra; and Heaton Amateurs, who originally played at St. Barnabas's Church Hall and who moved to the Elite Cinema in 1947 with a production of *The Mikado*.

It is fascinating to note the development of performers as actors and dancers. For example, in the early days of the societies, the ladies of the chorus were asked to do little else than look pretty, walk gracefully and wear beautiful clothes. Requirements of Edwardian-rooted musical comedies like *The Arcadians* and *The Quaker Girl* did not demand much more of them. For many chorus numbers, too, the women — *and* the men — stood in semi-circles or in a straight line to sing in the manner of a choir. But when the zip of the big American musical arrived, concentration on movement and characterisation had to be just as intense as that for the singing.

If you had told early members of Bradford's amateur operatic societies that one day their successors would be high-kicking with the discipline of acrobats and performing with great pace and agility in shows like *West Side Story,* they wouldn't have believed you.

Helping societies to advance so progressively have frequently been the interpretive powers of excellent local producers, like Peter Blakeney, Tony Haigh, Keith Marsden, Tony Cross and Kenneth Paine, and first-rate choreographers such as Queenie Roma and Patricia Ann Taylor. All have reward of knowing that they have brought pleasure to thousands.

Many of Bradford's major amateur operatic companies took advantage of not only the staging facilities of the Alhambra, but of the availability of the theatre within the nearby and comparatively new Central Library. Here were presented such extravaganzas as *The Merry Widow* and *The Pajama Game* — further proof of the remarkable spate of big amateur shows in the area.

Norah Blaney

To Bradford Amateurs fell the honour of having in the company an actress and revue star who only a few seasons before, in the 1920's, had been the toast of the West End and a friend of the Prince of Wales.

She was Norah Blaney who, with her partner, Gwen Farrar, wowed them in places like the Palladium and the Coliseum before their act broke up. Norah then became a celebrity of musical comedy and more sophisticated revue.

Francis Laidler engaged Norah to star with George Lacy in his first pantomime at the Alhambra, the 1930-31 *Mother Goose*. While in the city she met the Bradford surgeon Basil Hughes, married him and left the stage.

In 1933 Norah agreed to appear in what transpired to be one of the greatest-ever successes of the Bradford Amateurs — *The Vagabond King*. It had its audience on its feet cheering.

In the cast was a local actress who became one of Norah's best friends. She was Bessie Pratt who was so outstanding that not long afterwards she too was starring, as principal girl, in *Red Riding Hood* at the Alhambra. Bessie was so good that Laidler invited her to return as *Cinderella*.

During her days in the West Riding Norah Blaney lived in Baildon but returned to the London stage when her husband died in 1953. In 1960 she starred with Sybil Thorndike, Marie Lhör, Mary Clare and Graham Payne in Noel Coward's *Waiting in the Wings*. She also spent a season at the Royal Shakespeare Theatre at Stratford-upon-Avon and appeared in ITV's *Crossroads*. She died, aged ninety, in December 1983.

'State-of-the-art' lighting introduced to the Alhambra 1947.
Photograph taken in 1972. The operator is Fred Wade.

Olivier to the Rescue

"Ah! Bradford! Isn't that where Irving died?"

After the laughter had subsided in a room on London's South Bank, Britain's current leading knight of the stage was told not to worry. All signs were healthy for the National Theatre's first visit to the Alhambra where, later in the run, Sir Laurence Olivier was to portray the solicitor in Somerset Maugham's play, *Home and Beauty*.

"Well that's all right then," said Sir Laurence — but it turned out to be not quite all right, even if the National Theatre booking was certain of large audiences and was one of the most prestigious obtained by Rowland Hill. Not all right at the start anyway.

The National's Bradford dates were from March 10th to 15th, 1969. From the Monday to the Thursday the company was to present Sir Laurence's production of Chekhov's *Three Sisters,* with his wife Joan Plowright as Masha; and on the Friday and Saturday it was to stage three performances of *Home and Beauty.*

On the Monday morning, however, it was learned that Robert Stephens would not be able to play Vershinin in *Three Sisters,* for this Bradford-trained actor and associate director of the National was in bed with 'flu.

The outcome was that early on Monday afternoon Sir Laurence stepped from his shining blue Rolls Royce after it pulled up outside the Alhambra stage door at the end of a two-hundred-and-fifty-mile rescue dash. He had not planned to come to Bradford until the Friday because from Tuesday to Thursday he had to give four performances of the taxing role of the captain of artillery in Strindberg's *The Dance of Death* in London.

But on Monday the unflappable Sir Laurence sped north in his chauffeur-driven car. With him was Lady Olivier and the young actor chosen to take over the major role of Vershinin. He was Derek Jacobi, whose smaller role of Tusenbach was in turn taken over by Ronald Pickup.

Jacobi, whose portrayal of the emperor Claudius was to become a television classic, had neither played nor understudied Vershinin before, although he was familiar with the role through his appearance as Tusenbach. Sir Laurence and his wife drove from their Brighton home and picked Derek up in London. From there, during the long drive, Derek Jacobi rehearsed his new role coached by Sir Laurence.

They arrived at the Alhambra barely in time for a rehearsal called for 2 p.m.; and from then on for Sir Laurence it was almost non-stop work until 10.20 p.m. when there were seven curtain calls from a delighted audience. (I say until 10.20 because, even when the play was in performance, Sir Laurence was here, there and everywhere making sure everything was all right.)

Three Sisters was an exquisite production which highlighted the comedy within the play and the performance went off well. Understandably Derek Jacobi gave a somewhat muted performance — but he was to thrill Alhambra audiences some seasons later with a riveting *Hamlet.*

On the Monday night after the performance Sir Laurence went to stay at the Midland Hotel because its association with Irving fascinated him. Next morning he drove back to London, returning to Bradford on the Friday. In *Home and Beauty* he played the third-act role of Mr. A. B. Raham, a conniving solicitor, and once again proved his mastery of character creation. I don't recall having seen him in any other similar role where he exuded the oil of expediency in a way so winning that Shylock would have swapped his pound of flesh for an hour's tuition.

The Managers

So many people have given loyal, even loving service to the Alhambra that it is a pity they cannot all be mentioned in the book, people like Renee Reid who for many years was an extremely popular barmaid; Amy Hodgson, who worked in the office for nearly twenty years; Wilfred Calvert, the former head flyman and William Cadman, who designed and painted scenery for so many Laidler pantomimes ... There are dozens who merit remembering and Bradford theatregoers are much in their debt.

Because their contributions to the Alhambra were so vital, I must, however, name some of the theatre's managers and stage-managers.

Early on I mentioned the Alhambra's first manager, Walter Havers, who came to the theatre from Keighley Hippodrome. For many years he had been manager for Henry Ainley and then for Phyllis Neilson-Terry. He was also touring manager for Lillie Langtry, the Jersey Lillie. He began his career at seventeen giving impersonations of Henry Irving and other stars. He was the writer of some good pantomime scripts, including *Goody Two Shoes,* as well as being the author of some of the sketches used by Robb Wilton. He eventually joined Gilbert Miller, whose most important production at the time was *Monsieur Beaucaire.*

He was followed as manager by William Strannock who stayed for only a brief spell. Then in 1915, a man who was to become an Alhambra legend was appointed manager and remained so for twenty-nine years. He was Philip A. Lennon, a figure of imposing dignity and courtesy who did a great deal for charities. His wife, who had been a ballet dancer, used to hold little classes for the children of friends on a closed Alhambra stage. One of them was Queenie Roma who choreographed many Bradford shows and became a teacher herself.

Philip Lennon began his association with theatre when he was a schoolboy. He was a chorister at the Brompton Oratory, the choir which was often drawn upon to supply the chorus for grand opera at Covent Garden. After leaving school he received an appointment at the London Empire and in 1899, as manager, he opened the Bradford Empire. He stayed there for six years.

On Lennon's death in 1944 Francis Laidler appointed Fred Moore as manager of the Alhambra. He was no stranger to Bradford theatregoers, for he was appointed manager of the Bradford Palace in 1928 and remained there until 1937 when he became manager of the Halifax Palace.

Although Fred had a keen sense of humour he was not one for allowing artists to go "over the mark". The iron hand was there, and so was the blue-pencil.

"But it's my biggest laugh," said one comic of a dubious line which Moore wanted him to cut. "If I cut that out I may as well cut out the whole act." "Right," said Fred, "we'll cut out the whole act!"

Moore retired in May 1947 and his successor was Bradford-born George Baines who had been stage director for Laidler pantomimes in Bradford, Leeds, Sheffield and Bristol. George's starting salary was £16 a week, not an inconsiderable sum them. By December 1964, when he retired, his earnings in comparative value had dropped considerably — which gives an idea of the reductions some were prepared to accept in order to keep the Alhambra going.

George Baines was a theatre man through and through. He had started his career as a member of a juvenile concert party, then as half of a double act in Variety with his older brother. During the first World War he became a member of the Army concert party in Germany.

George Baines, father of BBC North TV announcer Brian Baines, was one of the Alhambra's most popular managers.

After his release from the forces he was associated with Rob Currie and later was stage manager for Leslie Henson. He had also been connected with Archie Pitt, Duggie Wakefield and Phil Strickland and Jack Hayes. He produced summer shows at the Central Pier, Blackpool, and it was there that Francis Laidler spotted him and booked him to appear in one of his pantomimes in Plymouth, thus starting a long association.

After the retirement of Rowland Hill, who for some time had had outstanding help from house-manager Allan Davey, the last management link with Laidler's Alhambra was the appointment as manager of Sydney Derrick who had been assistant secretary to Mr. Hill.

Sidney Derrick, a trained accountant, guided the Alhambra through some difficult times. "But I certainly think things have turned the corner and I'm sure provincial theatres have a viable future", he said when he took early retirement in 1983 after almost a decade as manager. "Though I would have loved to get involved with the computers and the new developments, I would not have been there long enough to see anything through. I felt it was the best thing to finish a career which I have enjoyed so much."

The Stage Managers

The Alhambra had hardly been opened in 1914 before Francis Laidler brought Johnny Hawkridge there as stage manager. He was still filling that position almost up to the moment of his death in December 1948, thirty four years later. All told, Johnny, a cigar-puffing character, had spent nearly fifty-six years of his life in the theatre.

He started as a call-boy at the Theatre Royal, Leeds, where he eventually became stage-manager. Among those to whom he had shouted "Overture and beginners, please" were Wilson Barrett, Edmund Tearle and many others of the old school of actor-managers.

Johnny was renowned for his immaculate bow-tied appearance when on duty. One Monday night when members of a revue chorus were making their first appearance, one of the girls saw him standing in the prompt box and asked who he was. When told he was the stage manager she exclaimed: "Good heavens! At the theatre we visited last week the stage manager wore a fisherman's jersey, chewed tobacco and was anything but polite." That, as an observer remarked, was the effect of Johnny's boiled shirt on hard-boiled chorus girls.

Johnny's sanctum was a little room beneath the stage. It was plastered with an incredible number of photographs given to him by performers. Practically every inch of the four walls was covered with them, and the desk drawers, too, were full to overflowing with portraits and snaps.

During the Second World War there were many people who were grateful to Johnny Hawkridge. He organised a concert party, *Highlights of Variety,* which gave hundreds of performances to the Forces all over the north of England and raised £2,000 for war charities.

Johnny's little room beneath the stage was also the home of Bert Tyas who succeeded him as stage manager. When Bert retired, in 1976 at the age of seventy-three, he had worked on more than 1,450 shows, including well over 150 major amateur operatic productions.

Mexborough-born Bert started a thirty-two years' association with Bradford theatre in 1944 when he was appointed stage manager and electrician at the Prince's Theatre. When he crossed the road to the Alhambra he was to work with hundreds of stars.

He was also responsible for introducing and creating much of the decor for the Variety shows of the fifties and early sixties. But the most demanding show he tackled was the visiting London production of *White Horse Inn* with its colossal on-stage revolve.

Of all the producers and directors he worked with, the man who most impressed Bert Tyas was his original Bradford boss, Francis Laidler. Said Bert: "He not only knew what he was about without ever showing temper, but was willing to listen to and accept suggestions: he was a real professional."

When Bert retired, Fred Wade, the Alhambra's electrician, was promoted to stage manager. Fred, who had also had experience at the Prince's in earlier days, worked not only on productions, but also to keep the Alhambra open. He it was who campaigned enthusiastically after the launching of the "Save-the-Alhambra" petition in early 1984. He was appointed collator by the Musicians' Union, the actors' union Equity and the National Association of Theatre Technicians and Kinematic Employees which together inaugurated the petition. Thousands of signatures came the way of Fred who had worked at the Alhambra for thirty-five years.

It was obvious that the company which made the film of Ronald Harwood's play, *The Dresser,* at the Alhambra — the last activity at the theatre before its re-opening — knew Fred's worth. In thanking him for his assistance, it featured his name prominently in the final credits, together with that of Paul Andrews, the then theatre manager.

Fred Wade (left) demonstrates the Alhambra's new lighting controls to singer John Hanson, 1974.

By Courtesy of Fred Wade.

89

The Proscenium of the old Alhambra Theatre.   *By Courtesy of the Yorkshire Post*

The Auditorium of the old Alhambra Theatre.   *By Courtesy of the Yorkshire Post*

Part Two

Bradford's 'New' Theatre

Nightfall

On Monday, May 27th, 1974, the final Alhambra presentation under the Rowland Hill banner opened for a week's run. Starring Paul Massie and *Coronation Street's* Peter Adamson, it was a psychological thriller called *Nightfall.*

Is the title prophetic? — that was the obvious question. Was this going to be the beginning of the end of the theatre, or the start of a new beginning? Whatever was to happen, the Alhambra would never be the same. The last direct connection with the Laidlers was being severed and henceforth the theatre would not only be owned by the city, but would be run by it.

Although Rowland Hill retired on Saturday, June 1st, he was back in the theatre the next night with his wife for a concert given in his honour by the massed ranks of Bradford's leading amateur operatic companies.

It was a moving occasion — so much so that Rowland Hill described it as "the greatest night of my career". He struck a serious note when he told the packed audience: "By all means support the amateur productions but support the professional productions as well. For without the professionals this theatre will die."

There were to be many times during the next decade when it seemed that his plea had failed. Yet was the public really to blame for its indifference? As a council-run theatre the Alhambra confronted serious problems. Star entertainers were almost entirely monopolised by the club circuits; to most of those who toured big productions it was as though the Alhambra didn't exist; the pop scene was still strong and keeping young people away; and a preponderance of middle-of-the-road plays could not be a box-office magnet because Bradford always refused to regard the Alhambra as principally a playhouse.

It was a huge headache therefore which awaited Ron Cussons in December 1976, when he joined Bradford Metro as its principal entertainments officer. Brought up in Harrogate and with a wide experience of cinema management behind him, Cussons came to Bradford from Southport where he had improved the status of live entertainment significantly.

Almost immediately Mr. Cussons noted two important factors: that the annual pantomime would have to make more money if the Alhambra was to survive; and that, if ever top-star attractions did become available, the theatre with intensive promotion would have to draw audiences from a large catchment area. It was also vital that the Alhambra should be enlarged and modernised if the big stars were going to include the theatre in their itineraries.

It was 1981, however, before Mr. Cussons could really begin to implement some of his ambitions. Even so, bookings for that year included Jack Jones, Freddie Starr, *The Wayne Sleep Show,* Tommy Steele, Mike Harding and the play *Middle-aged Spread,* with Frank Windsor and Trevor Bannister.

The prospect for the Alhambra, following a smash-hit Cannon and Ball pantomime, was the most encouraging for years. Les Dawson, Little and Large, The Krankies, Bill Maynard and Russ Abbot were some of those who made it possible for the Alhambra to be publicised as *The Home of Panto in the North.*

When the capable and astute Ron Cussons arrived in Bradford, the annual panto was grossing nowhere near enough. By the time he left in the spring of 1986, to become Eastbourne's director of tourism and leisure, he had upped the figure to £500,000.

There was a cold reception outside when Little and Large arrived at the Alhambra in December 1981 to start pantomime rehearsals. But their show was to radiate much warmth and friendliness. The pair were among the keenest campaigners for the preservation of the Bradford theatre.

Between the old and the new

The years between Rowland Hill's retirement and the "new" Alhambra had several highlights apart from the pantomime — although early on in that period it looked as if there might not be any at all.

The setback came with *Pygmalion.* Many of the public at that time might have preferred to see Shaw's classic comedy dolled up as *My Fair Lady* judging by the bookings which were alarmingly small — in spite of a cast which included Evelyn Laye, Paul Daneman, Bill Owen and Jennifer Wilson, and Val May's superlative production.

The young impresario Vanessa Ford brought Shakespeare's *The Merchant of Venice,* and in subsequent years presented increasingly impressive productions of the classics including an admirable *Macbeth* in which the title role was played with memorable clarity by Douglas Fielding. Vanessa Ford's achievement in mounting these productions without any subsidy was remarkable, and one which otherwise would have left the Alhambra starved of major drama.

One of the best performances of the decade was by Joanna Lumley in Noel Coward's *Private Lives,* staged in an accomplished production by James Roose-Evans. Other fine productions included *There's a Girl in My Soup,* with John Stride and Debbie Arnold; *The Secretary Bird,* with Hayley Mills; *Same Time Next Year* with Diane Keen and Ray Lonnen; Fenella Fielding in *Gigi* (the play, not the musical); and *The Mating Game,* with Barbara Windsor, Peggy Mount and Norman Vaughan.

Barbara Murray and Simon Ward starred in the thriller, *House Guest,* by Francis Durbridge who, fifty years earlier had decided to be a writer after buying every second-hand book he could afford from the stalls of Bradford's Swan Arcade and Kirkgate Market. Francis Durbridge was then a pupil for two years at Bradford Grammar School.

One oddity that appeared in September 1982 was a production of Agatha Christie's *The Hollow* in which Mandy Rice-Davies, famous for her part in the political scandals of the sixties, made a bid to establish herself as a straight actress.

It wasn't of course, all plays and pantomimes during this period. There were many attractions for those who enjoyed musical entertainment — like the voices of the great Tony Bennett and Charles Aznavour; the superb jazz violin of Stephan Grappelli, the exhilirating trumpet of Humphrey Lyttelton and the spectacular stagings of Northern Ballet Theatre and *The Rocky Horror Show.* There was glamour too, when Diana Dors, squeezed into a long black velvet gown, stood in the Alhambra spotlight. Nobody pretended she was the world's best songstress (certainly she didn't), but there was in her performance a magnetic artistry in pointing a line and under-scoring a deep-meaning phrase. And her moments as a raconteur were a delectable blend of the ribald and the elegant.

On the whole, though, the big touring productions were obviously absent. The Alhambra's staging facilities were no longer considered adequate by those who owned or presented these productions.

The Dresser

The 1980-81 Cannon and Ball pantomime was followed by two more highly successful pantos — *Aladdin,* with Little and Large and *Cinderella,* with Russ Abbot (during its run he won a national entertainer-of-the-year award).

But before the final pantomime at the "old" theatre, the Alhambra became a temporary film studio when it was chosen as the central setting for the British film, *The Dresser,* adapted from his own play by Ronald Harwood. Set against a background of wartime Britain, *The Dresser* was about a grandiloquent actor-manager known simply as 'Sir' (played by Albert Finney) who had given his very soul to his theatrical career, often at the expense of those closest to him.

Pivotal to 'Sir's' existence was Norman, his loyal dresser, played by Tom Courtenay. Norman was equally passionate about the theatre and dedicated to his master, but he was nevertheless wryly aware of his chief's frequently unreasonable demands.

The Alhambra was chosen as the principal location because it was considered ideal for the story's backstage portrayal of the life and relationships within an old-time touring stage company. It was selected during a pre-production reconnaissance trip to the north of England in which Albert Finney and Tom Courtenay took part in order to "get the feel of treading the boards in the right kind of atmosphere".

The man who insisted on this was the film's director, Peter Yates, whose previous successes included *Bullitt* and *The Deep.* Film-making at the Alhambra went on for many days and the outcome was an outstanding film which not only got five Oscar nominations and won prizes, but which also preserved on film for posterity just what the stage and auditorium of the "old" Alhambra looked like.

The film unit, the players and the author all made many friends in Bradford which provided numerous extras for the film. They were so delighted by the co-operation they received from the city that in March 1984, when *The Dresser* was on release, the cast presented a showcase to the Alhambra containing photographs and a thanks-to-Bradford message.

Director Peter Yates told the gathering that not only was the film company grateful to Bradford, but it was also overjoyed that the Alhambra was to be saved and developed. Theatres like the Alhambra, he said, were essential to the nation's well-being and provided vital places for actors to perfect their craft.

The location filming of *The Dresser* preluded the last pantomime at the "old" Alhambra. It was *Babes in the Wood,* starring The Krankies, Billy Dainty, Peter Goodwright, Alan Curtis and Janet Edis, and was a big success. It took its final bow on the first Saturday of March, 1984, and was both a sad and happy occasion — sad because so much was being said farewell to, happy because the news was out that the Alhambra was saved and would re-open after vast improvements and refurbishment.

Stars who had campaigned for the Alhambra's salvation — including Sir Laurence Olivier, Beryl Grey, Billie Whitelaw, Leslie Sands, John Hanson, Mike Harding, Little and Large, and many more — must have felt like cheering when they heard of the Council's decision.

On the final night of *Babes in the Wood* the cast also took the opportunity to express their relief and pleasure. The Krankies said: "We are particularly pleased that the Council has taken notice of public opinion." (They were referring to the mammoth response to the petition co-ordinated by Alhambra stage-manager, Fred Wade), and Peter Goodwright added: "I'm delighted by the Council's wise decision."

Most expansive was comedian Billy Dainty. He had every right to be so because as a Variety veteran he personified what so much of the "old" Alhambra had been about.

Thank Heaven for the EEC

In any discussion about the saving and redevelopment of the Alhambra, one observation demands to be made. It is that there should be no derision aimed at those who were against spending millions of pounds on the theatre.

With vast unemployment all round, with industry starved of investment, with health and welfare services desperate for money to help the needy in a society with longer life expectancy, with old school buildings almost falling apart and with pitted highways crying out for repairs, it was a brave councillor who was prepared to advocate spending money on a theatre.

How could he or she convince voters that the modernisation of the Alhambra might attract thousands of visitors and thus not only improve Bradford's image but bring into the city some much needed cash?

Those in favour of an improved Alhambra had one excellent debating point, however. It was that Bradford, with its new, magnificent and well-supported National Museum of Photography, Film and Television, had decided to develop as a tourist centre and, to many people's surprise — even astonishment — had done so successfully. Wouldn't it be an odd tourist centre without an adequate top-class entertainment showcase?

Even so, it isn't every day a provincial city renovates, rejuvenates and improves with splendour a local theatre so that its stage and audience facilities are better than some of the best in London's West End. Happily, there are those who saw such refurbishing of the Alhambra as a sound investment which might soon have all Bradfordians blessing its originators.

This argument, more an outcome of Yorkshire common-sense than of artistic ambition, didn't really take into account the yearnings of Thespis. But it could have, because ever since the days of Ancient Greece communities purporting to be civilised have considered theatre a vital communal platform for the expressing and sharing of humanity's thoughts, dreams, ideas, ideals, aspirations, joys, sorrows, tragedies and comic quirks. This ethos has long been cherished on the Continent where, after the bombings of the Second World War, it was not unknown for some cities to rebuild their theatres even before famous churches.

More practically, however, those advocating that the Alhambra should be saved noted that within an hours' drive or train journey the theatre had a potential six million possible patrons. It was concluded that if attractions proved sufficiently prestigious, spectacular, star-studded or significant, people of the catchment area might flock to Bradford. In the north, theatres in Manchester and Hull had already proved that this kind of policy worked.

There were those who realised too that if the Alhambra, with its declining safety and sanitary standards, were not refurbished extensively it would die, both structurally and financially. Much of its accommodation and equipment, its facilities and amenities, were so antiquated or run down that it would all have spiralled, along with the audiences, into a creaking demise.

The Alhambra was left with only two options; go out of existence because of dilapidation and lack of shows, or modernise so effectively that No. 1 attractions and theatre lovers from a wide area would be eager to breathe new life into the enterprise. There were to be many arguments and objections before the city decided on the second choice.

Regarding plans to go ahead, some schemes were more grandiose than others and consequently estimates varied by millions. For a time there were hopes that the Government would give direct help to the refurbishment, but these were dashed when the Arts Minister, Lord Gowrie, said: "It is very much a matter for local councillors. It would be very difficult if we were involved in an enormous number of local decisions and there would be an incentive to local authorities to let everything go and say that the Government would pick up the bill.''

The agonising over the Alhambra's future was reflected in some of the newspaper headlines of the time: Shock Warning Over City Theatre ... Alhambra Must Be Subsidised

... Fight Is On To Save The Alhambra ... Alhambra Facing Another Blow ... Alhambra Future Looks Assured ... Alhambra's Big Improvement Scheme To Be Shelved ... Yes To £7½m Theatre Plan ... MP Says Scrap Alhambra Scheme ... Alhambra In Suspense ... Will Alhambra Get Kiss Of Life?

Fortunately, the answer to that final question was 'yes' — and it came not from the London corridors of power, but from across the North Sea. The headline anticipating this read: Alhambra's EEC Cash Quest.

It was followed two months later, in February 1984, by the news that a top-level all-party delegation of Bradford's political leaders was off to Brussels in a bid to find a cash lifeline for the Alhambra. A brochure setting out the case for aid had been prepared and would be handed to officials of the European Commission.

The delegation had been greatly encouraged by the enthusiasm of West Yorkshire Euro MP, Barry Seal, who had said: "Although there is limited cash available, I've argued strongly that EEC money couldn't be spent on a more vital project. I can guarantee that a delegation from Bradford will see the people that matter in Brussels."

The delegation, comprising Tory deputy leader, Councillor Ronnie Farley, Labour leader Councillor Philip Beeley and Liberal leader Councillor Paul Hockney, spent two days in Belgium and were delighted to report when they returned that they had got the go-ahead to submit their bid for Euro cash for the Alhambra.

They had been accompanied by Chief Executive Gordon Moore and Peter Redfern from the Policy Unit and Mark Foster from the Bradford Economic Development Unit, which was to win special gratitude for the sterling work done by Ian Page, the project co-ordinator for the refurbished Alhambra.

Principal entertainments officer Ron Cussons too, must have felt like waving a flag because he had fought tooth and nail, (sometimes almost to the point of illness), to bring the "new" Alhambra to fruition.

That "new" Alhambra was to cost £8.2m — £2.1m from the EEC without whose help the Alhambra almost certainly would have become derelict.

As it was, the first 'stars' of the "new" Alhambra were able to move in quickly — 170 of them! No-one asked for their autographs and the only 'make-up' they wore was of streaks of cement or dust on hands and brow. Their 'costumes' comprised little more than dirty jeans or crumpled drills, offset by the brightness of their safety helmets.

The valiant 170 were, of course, the workforce who, almost on schedule, completed the "new" Alhambra in time for its opening season, starting on Tuesday, May 27th 1986, with a visit by the Ballet Rambert.

Understandably the Clerk of Works, Jack Webster, was proud of his work-force, especially because, except for electrical and mechanical specialists, most of it was recruited from the Bradford area.

The Lord Mayor of Bradford, Councillor Mohammed Ajeeb, formally marked the end of the structural rebuilding work in a topping-out ceremony in August 1985 and news of the reconstruction progress had travelled swiftly.

There was the ticket collector at London's King's Cross Station, for example. "Have they nearly finished the Alhambra yet" he asked an amazed David Wright, the site architect, after noticing that David (whom he didn't know) was travelling to Bradford.

The question was further evidence of how interest in the Alhambra had extended far beyond the boundaries of Bradford. London and Brussels were among those fascinated, as was the whole of live theatre. Francis Laidler had left a bigger heritage than he realised, even in his wildest dreams.

100

Bradford's Lord Mayor, Mohammed Ajeeb and his wife at the Topping-Out
Ceremony on the Bradford Alhambra, August 1985.
Tom Brailsford, executive director of Higgs and Hill, is on the left.

The Right Mixture

"Of all the theatres we have designed or refurbished, the Alhambra has presented particular problems in resolving the mixture of new and old building. During construction we were never quite certain what we would find as the place was opened up; and, in a design sense, each area has been a "one-off" — every decision involving careful consideration of how Edwardian or how modern the detail should be. It is most encouraging to wander among the audience in the foyers before a show and hear the generally favourable response from all age groups. Bradford certainly seems to be taking the new Alhambra to its bosom."

These are the words of Robin Derham who, with Nicholas Thompson, is a partner of the London-based leading theatre architects Renton Howard Wood Levin Partnership (RHWL). Mr. Derham, a man of sincerity, charm and great skill, was from the start determined that nothing should impair the Alhambra's intrinsic character, for he loves theatre and that affection is reflected in his own and his colleagues' achievement.

RHWL now has an unrivalled reputation in the building or refurbishment of theatres and other types of auditoria. Among its successes are the Sheffield Crucible, the London Old Vic, Nottingham Theatre Royal, London's Duke of York Theatre, the Newcastle Theatre Royal, Brighton Dome and Warwick Arts Centre.

Before the twenty-one month building programme began the Alhambra had barely been altered since it was built in 1914. "It remained almost a museum piece, but a number of crucial deficiencies were seriously threatening its future," commented the architects. "The remarkably fine and intact auditorium was let down by a totally sub-standard stage, backstage, administrative and sanitary accommodation. Furthermore, the existing foyers were virtually non-existent, since patrons originally entered their respective tiers from the street via a series of independent stair towers."

RHWL's feasibility study, commissioned by Bradford Metropolitan Council in November 1982, showed that by selective surgery and the construction of new additions this Grade II listed building could meet not only the expectations of late twentieth-century audiences, but also the requirements of performers and the aspirations of the Council to ensure the highest possible degree of commercial viability.

The feasibility report recommended the immediate acquisition of the Majestic Cinema at the rear of the Alhambra to permit a major increase in the main stage depth and the creation of much needed rehearsal/studio space. The study also indicated that a reduction in the carriageway of the adjoining Great Horton Road could make way for major front-of-house and backstage facilities.

Higgs and Hill Building Limited were appointed as Management Contractors in December 1983 and the project finally received the delayed go-ahead for a site start in August 1984.

The beautiful auditorium required highly specialised modernisation and was lavishly redecorated in a range of gilts and subtle shades of warm reds, with white and blue highlighting the tier fronts and boxes. Carpets were specially designed and the existing high-level paintings were magnificently restored.

Boxes and control rooms inserted at the rear worked effectively with the decorative scheme to increase the sense of intimacy in the 1,500 seat auditorium.

Externally the famous three domes were retained with the forward rotunda containing a glazed grand staircase enabling the audience to be seen from the outside as they make their way between the new foyer levels within.

An entirely new entrance front was created together with a double height entrance hall which includes all public amenities, a shop and computerised box-office. A mezzanine gallery overlooking the entrance hall links the "pit bar" and its eating area with the grand staircase and the stalls lobby — a small, ornate foyer which previously contained the dress-circle stairs.

Two generous upper foyer levels, with broad coffered ceilings and island bars, now give access to the upper tiers through new routes inserted beneath the auditorium raked seating — thereby minimising the ascent by stairs. The foyers were designed to provide a community meeting place, open throughout the day and with enough space for occasional lunchtime entertainments. The disabled were provided with designated toilets and a level route from the street giving access to the "pit bar" and the stalls, where removeable seats (all now on "Continental" spacings) may accommodate wheelchairs.

The stage area was doubled in depth — from thirty feet to sixty feet — and a completely new flytower was constructed, with more than fifty-five counterweight sets. The flat, lightly sprung stage floor, greatly enlarged orchestra pit (in two sections), ample wing space for "run-offs" and good links to the full-sized rehearsal space made the Alhambra particular attractive for all forms of dance as well as musicals, ambitious pantomimes and other large-scale productions.

The rehearsal-studio space within the Old Majestic Cinema — known as the Alhambra Studio — underwent a complete transformation to provide an auditorium for up to four hundred people for musical and theatrical events, community functions and exhibitions. It is possible for the two auditoria both to be used for certain events, including conferences.

The original backstage accommodation was totally re-planned and re-equipped with new extensions on three levels to provide additional dressing-rooms, wardrobe, showers, assembly area and get-in. The administration floor on the top has access to the studio as well as to the main theatre.

The Laidler Club room, with its own lounge bar, is located between backstage and front-of-house to accommodate either public or performance-related events and it houses the Laidler commemorative plaque, unveiled by Val Parnell in 1956, as well as numerous mementoes and photographs evocative of the Alhambra's past.

The new Alhambra project set out to reinforce visually the very best of the existing building and to harmonise it with the new work, which is itself a careful blend of Edwardian and modern themes. Many of the original features and period characteristics were translated delightfully into the language and materials of the 1980's.

Gala Opening of
The Jewel of Bradford

As had been planned, the spectacularly refurbished Alhambra first housed an audience on Tuesday, May 27th, 1986, and it was a night to remember. So that all teething troubles could be overcome, the official gala opening of the theatre had been fixed to take place at the end of October.

Nevertheless, that initial evening had such a splendour about it that all those fortunate enough to be there knew immediately that they were attending a great occasion — not only for Bradford, but for a large part of northern England and even for theatre nationally.

Still capped by its distinctive domes, the Alhambra, as nearly everyone present noted (including television cameramen, a large number of journalists and critics, and many dignitaries and celebrities) had been transformed magnificently into the Jewel of Bradford.

The Alhambra Refurbishers

Client: City of Bradford Metropolitan Council.

Project Co-ordinator: Ian Page

Architects: Renton Howard Wood Levin Partnership.
Partners: Robin Derham, Nicholas Thompson.

Job Architect: Christine Leyland

Site Architect: David Wright

Architectural team: Nigel Higgs, Tony Hudson, Steve Tucker, John Walsom

Advisers: Barry Pritchard, Tony Williams

Auditoriums: Clare Ferraby in consultation with Terence Whitwell, architect to City of Bradford MC

Clerk of Works: Employed by Bradford MC — Jack Webster, Steve Barber

Consulting Engineers: Ove Arup and Partners (structural, mechanical, electrical and lift installations)

Quantity Surveyors: Gleeds, Nottingham

Specialist Consultants: Theatre Projects Consultant Ltd. theatrical equipment including stage rigging, production and working lighting, and sound and communications installations

Main Contractor: Higgs and Hill Building Ltd.

REHEARSAL STUDIO: The rehearsal studio is contained in what was formerly the Majestic Cinema. This was generally a low key refurbishment of the existing property, with the installation of new services, plant rooms and boilerhouse serving the whole of the Alhambra complex.

London Festival Ballet's exquisite production of Coppelia was the attraction at the 'new' Alhambra's gala opening.

Exclamations of delight came from more than a thousand throats as first-nighters relaxed comfortably in the reception area and in the spacious bars during the two intervals of a programme presented by Ballet Rambert.

Even more spectacular was the official gala opening of the new Alhambra on Thursday night, October 30th, 1986.

Not only did the auditorium look gorgeous, with its florally decorated boxes and its packed audience in evening dress, but there was an international atmosphere thanks to the presence, as principal guest of honour, of France's Monsieur Jacques Delors, president of the Commission of the European Communities. He it was who unveiled a commemorative plaque and through him Bradford's thanks were taken to the EEC for the financial help it had given the Alhambra.

Councillor Barry Thorne, chairman of the Council's Leisure Services Committee, said in an introductory welcome that he was determined that the "superb Alhambra" would continue to belong to the people of the city, while Mr. Giles Shaw, MP for Pudsey and Minister for Trade and Industry, told the assembly that the Alhambra showed what was possible with co-operation between different groups, both in Bradford's political scene and throughout the EEC.

Among the other VIPs were Bradford's Lord Mayor and Lady Mayoress, Councillor and Mrs. Bill Nunn; the leader of the Council, Councillor Phil Beeley; City Recreation Officer, Howell Williams; Councillor Ronnie Farley, Opposition Leader of Bradford Council; Gordon Moore, the Council's Chief Executive and, appropriately, Bradford's Euro MP, Barry Seal.

From the stage, actor Frazer Hines spoke the words of a specially written prologue to mark the occasion — and the curtain went up on a sparkling performance of *Coppelia* by London Festival Ballet.

The production, directed by Ronald Hynd, was an ideal choice for such a festive night, for not only did it provide superb entertainment, but it utilised to the full some of the most impressive features of the refurbished theatre — the large stage, the huge orchestra pit and the computerised lighting equipment.

During the evening Monsieur Delors observed that while providing a cultural focus for the future, Bradford had preserved the best features of the Alhambra's past.

"And a glorious past it was," he continued. "I know of the history of this theatre and its founder, Francis Laidler. He was a great man. He helped shape the theatrical traditions of this city and under his guiding light the years between the wars especially were great years. On the Continent I have heard too of how those who picked up the torch found themselves faced with increasing problems. I've heard also of the struggle to maintain audiences against the challenges of new leisure preferences, new fashions and new tastes.

"I am aware too of the stalwart efforts of Rowland Hill and his dedicated and talented professionals who kept this theatre alive with equipment which was becoming increasing outmoded ...

"At the theatre tonight we are celebrating a relaunch, a new *elan,* with the well-grounded optimism of those who know that they have adapted the old to meet the needs of the future. The European Community has, I am glad to say, been able to make its contribution."

Rowland Hill was seated in the audience and of the Alhambra's refurbishments he remarked: "All I can say is that I am delighted with what has happened. It is magnificent. It will carry on gaining a reputation as one of the country's finest theatres well into the next century and I only wish I had more years left to live to see it flourish."

His love of the Alhambra clearly remained as great as it was during the heyday of his old boss, Francis Laidler.

Next day, on Friday, October 31st, I was with Rowland Hill at the unveiling of the J. B. Priestley statue, just opposite the Alhambra. The unveiling was carried out by J. B.'s widow, Jacquetta Hawkes, who had been present at the previous night's gala performance.

Afterwards, while strolling by the City Hall, Rowland reflected on Priestley's connections with Laidler's Alhambra. Then, smiling wryly, he whispered: "Do you know something? I didn't even get a mention in Francis Laidler's will."

The New Governor

For all the splendour of its improvements it was obvious throughout the theatre world that if the good ship Alhambra was to sail confidently and safely through the years ahead it was essential that a highly accomplished and experienced captain was at the helm.

In Peter Tod it found one. Within days of his being appointed the Alhambra's administrator his entrepreneurial flair, balanced by an appetite for the best the modern stage can offer, gave the Alhambra the confidence of knowing just where it was going.

"Only the best productions must play Bradford," he declared emphatically. "We must be the leader and not a pale imitation of other theatres in the region. While here, my only intention is to bat for Bradford," he added with a will which could match that of Ian Botham bent on knocking hell out of the Aussies.

Peter Tod made his first theatrical entrance in 1969 when he became an assistant administrator at Hull's New Theatre. He has run theatres throughout the country and two of them — Darlington Civic Theatre and the Bristol Hippodrome — he revived and transformed into major showcases.

Although 41 year-old Mr. Tod left the Alhambra to become supremo of the Birmingham Hippodrome in late 1988, he had in two short years established the Bradford theatre as a regional treasure.

It was he, for example, who persuaded the great London Festival Ballet (which was soon to become the English National Ballet) to make the Alhambra its northern 'home' for at least five years. And he was much involved in plans to make Bradford the National Theatre's northern base.

Because of him too, major pre-London stagings like the world premiere of Natalia Makarova's *Swan Lake,* and the Royal Shakespeare's Company's *Kiss Me, Kate,* became not uncommon. And Peter was there too to acknowledge a Royal patronage visit by Princess Margaret.

Mr. Tod's Bradford stay might have been comparatively short; but the lead he gave to the Alhambra and the entrepreneurial foundation he laid will endure. No better example could have been given to his successor.

Parade of Pleasure

"Have you ever seen such a beautiful theatre in your life?"

With a sweep of arms Tommy Steele asked this of a capacity audience as he launched into his new one-man show at the Alhambra to mark his thirtieth year in show business. He was obviously overjoyed and he went on to confirm, with dazzling ability, that he is one of the few Cockney sparrers who have been able to have northern audiences cheering.

His admiration for the Alhambra was soon to be endorsed by many other performers; and the parade of shows they appeared in reflected Peter Tod's awareness that the

Alhambra could not sit back on its modernisation laurels. Bums on seats — preferably on all seats — was paramount, and shows had to have a balanced and widespread appeal.

And, so it proved, they had. It soon became a commonplace event to attract bookings from scores of miles away. It was not unknown for parties to travel from as far away as Berkshire, Hertfordshire, Northumbria and even Scotland.

Big-scale musicals like *Jesus Christ Superstar, The Sound of Music, The Muppet Show* and *Peter Pan* were all enthusiastically received. So, too, by a different kind of audience, was a huge new production of *The Rocky Horrow Show.* Dressed in all manner of weird and erotic attire, the predominantly young audience, helping to consolidate the show as a cult, were even more fascinating than the harmlessly outrageous performers.

I felt much more at home among the children who flocked to see the large-scale stagings of C. S. Lewis's delightful *The Lion, The Witch and The Wardrobe,* presented by the Vanessa Ford Company. They later returned with well-attended productions of *King Lear,* with Nigel Davenport, and *The Importance of Being Earnest* in a superb production with Jon Finch as Jack Worthing and Pauline Jameson as Lady Bracknell.

Gilbert and Sullivan lovers were happily catered for by a novel staging of *The Mikado* by the new Sadler's Wells Opera Company. It was directed by Bradford-born Chris Pickles and featured another Bradfordian, Martin McEvoy, as Ko-Ko. The production, which incorporated many updatings of line, business and costume, concentrated its main satirical leg-pulling on a send-up of the British Empire under Queen Victoria. To bolster this was a Nanki-Poo played memorably as a Hoorey Henry by Christopher Gilbert.

When the Alhambra acquired the stage version, before its West End opening, of the television comedy series *'Allo, 'Allo,* it was as if a war for tickets had been declared. The box-office was besieged by thousands almost fighting to book seats.

And in the eyes of nearly everyone who managed to get into the show this send-up of stiff-upper-lip war films went down a bomb. The biggest cheers were for Gorden Kaye as Rene, the bungling cafè proprietor, for he had started his career as an amateur at the Bradford Playhouse.

In some respects, after many years, Music-hall had returned to the Alhambra, for in stage form *'Allo, 'Allo* comprised a series of comic sketches similar to those once common in Music-hall and revue.

Three other artists of television fame share an affinity with music-hall and Variety and also sparked a rush of support at the Alhambra. They are Rowan Atkinson and Cannon and Ball, all of whom would have topped Variety bills in the old days.

At Christmas, 1986, Cannon and Ball were delighted to have the honour of starring in the first pantomime to be produced at the reopened Alhambra: in *Babes in the Wood* they played to packed audiences for more than two months, supported by a marvellous Dame from Wyn Calvin.

That *Babes in the Wood* became the most successful pantomime in the Alhambra's history, being seen by 130,000 people in ten-and-a-half weeks. This was 13,000 more than the previous attendance record achieved by a Russ Abbot pantomime, even though the theatre's seating capacity had been reduced since then.

During the run 69,000 ice-creams, 25,000 programmes and 10,000 orange drinks were sold. And Cannon and Ball took a pasting in their slapstick scenes — by suffering the impact of more than 500 custard pies!

The most prestigious booking of the initial season was the Royal Shakespeare Company's production of Cole Porter's greatest musical, *Kiss Me, Kate.* Directed by Adrian Noble and starring Nichola McAuliffe, Paul Jones, Fiona Hendley, Tim Flavin, John Bardon and Emil Wolk *Kiss Me, Kate* was the epitome of the kind of big-scale professional musical that Alhambra audiences had been starved of for years. Packed houses gave it thunderous ovations.

Those same patrons were delighted when, after *Kiss Me, Kate* had transferred to the Savoy Theatre in the West End, Ms. McAuliffe won the award for best actress in a musical, and Bardon and Wolk, as the comic gangsters in the show, shared the best actor in a musical honour.

Many lustrous Alhambra productions were to follow. There was Bradford's own Kiki Dee marvellous in Willy Russell's *Blood Brothers,* for example; and Rowan Atkinson, an instant Alhambra favourite, established himself as an admirable comedy actor (as against a stand-up comic) in *The Sneeze.*

The list could be lengthy. Of the main highlights, however, I must recall the National Theatre's production of Tennessee Williams's *Cat On a Hot Tin Roof* (with Lindsay Duncan, Ian Charleson and Eric Porter); the Royal Shakespeare Company's *Hamlet* (with Mark Rylance) which was remarkably attuned to 20th century psychology; and, of course, Natalia Makarova's *Swan Lake* for the London Festival Ballet. Ms. Makarova, not only one of Russia's great dancers, but one of the greatest of the century anywhere, made many Bradford friends, all eager to welcome her back.

Her *Swan Lake* at the Alhambra was a world premiere and was seen by Princess Margaret, so adding to the list of Royal visitors who have visited the theatre, including Princess Anne (in 1977), the Duke of Edinburgh (in 1969) and Edward VIII when he was Prince of Wales (in 1929).

With regality the note, it is an appropriate moment to ring down the curtain on this Alhambra history. But it is not the end of the story. Not by any means. All signs point to a long and happy future.

In May 1989 Bradford Council appointed the Alhambra's supremo successor to Peter Tod. She was 41-year-old Anamaria Wills who, as its theatre director, had done wonders for the new Towngate Theatre in Basildon, Essex, an £8,500,000 new town enterprise.

The daughter of a much travelled technical manager with British Airways, Ms. Wills had taken a long and varied route to West Yorkshire — Montivideo in Uruguay, Peru, Bermuda, Karachi, Beirut, Tehran, New York, London, and, of course, Basildon.

In 1983 Ms. Wills, married to the technical manager of the new Towngate who, to his credit, insisted his wife should try for the Bradford post which would make her head of the entire Bradford Council Central Theatres complex, including the St. George's Hall, was appointed head of the marketing department of the National Theatre, South Bank, London. This was to prove a happy coincidence because the 'new' Alhambra quickly established a strong bond with the NT.

Ms. Wills, the mother of two youngsters, was called Anamaria because Uruguay, where she was born, insisted that children born in that country should be christened with at least one Spanish name.

That such a gifted woman should be put in charge of the Alhambra was exhilarating news for all those who believe women are as good as men any day!

Although so much is promised ahead, we nevertheless should not allow the Alhambra's new eminence to blind us to bygone years. The Alhambra's past is a remarkable past as tens of thousands of long gone patrons would have confirmed. They found their lives touched and enhanced by the Alhambra's magic.

By an architectural marvel the improvements, extensions and general modernisation have not robbed the Alhambra of its original character. Instead, they complement it magnificently. Because of this the phantoms have not fled. If you listen hard enough, you might just catch the sound of a crash of cymbals during some long-gone overture, or just hear the echo of spectral laughter and applause.

In the ornate, plaster-encrusted auditorium, beneath the Domes of Delight, the spirits of a host of entertainers perform on — the tumbling clowns, the graceful ballerinas, the soulful actors, the outrageous comics, the human nightingales, the cheeky chappies, the lavishly dressed and the scantily clad, the strapping principal boys ... All of them, and more, are atmospherically there.

And as the years pass their numbers will swell — for as long as the Alhambra is there to attract the cream of theatrical entertainment and the support of the public.

INDEX

Compiled by R. J. Duckett

This index includes all people, buildings, performers and shows directly related to the Bradford area and Francis Laidler's enterprises. Excluded are authors, playwrights, song titles, and names in the illustrative panels. Theatres and other buildings are entered under their name, not place, for example, Hippodrome, Keighley.

Index

115

Wall, Max, *comedian* 80
Wallace, Nellie, *singer-comedienne* 14
Walmsley, Fred, *actor* 21
Ward, Dorothy, *principal boy* 65
Ward, Polly, *actress* 35
Ward, Simon, *actor* 97
Warner, Jack, *actor* 46
Warriss, Ben, *comedian* 77
Waterhouse, Keith, *playwright* 80-81
Waters, Elsie and Doris, *comediennes* 46
Watson, Mamie, *actress* 14, 38
Watson, William, *architect* 10
Waxman, Al, *actor* 74
Wayne Sleep Show, dance entertainment 95
Webb, Alan, *actor* 79
Webb, Maurice, *Bradford M.P.* 34
Webster, Jack, *Clerk of Works* 100
Wedding in Paris, musical 30, 53
Welchman, Harry, *singer* 54
West End development, Bradford 1
West Yorkshire Savoyards Appreciation
  Society 53
Western Brothers, *comedian-pianists* 46
Whelan, Albert, *variety star* 77
When You're Young, musical 54
The Whip, play 4
White Horse Inn, musical 53, 88
Whitelaw, Billie, *actress* 81, 98
Whitfield, David, *singer* 80
Whittaker, Billy, *panto star* 67, 70
Wild Violets, musical 53
Williams, Howell, *recreation officer* 106
Williams, Oswald, *illusionist* 17-18

Wilson, Keppel and Betty, *comedy dance
  act* 69
Wilson, Jennifer, *actress* 97
Wilton, Robb, *actor-comedian* 46, 77, 86
Windsor, Barbara, *actress* 97
Windsor, Frank, *actor* 95
Winstone, Ruby, *actress* 33
Wise, Ernie, *actor-comedian* 50
Wiseman, Ernest (Ernie Wise) *actor-
  comedian* 50
Wolfe, J. H. *writer* 33
Wolk, Emil, *actor* 109
Wood, 'Wee' Georgie, *comedian* 47, 69, 77
Woodhead, Frank, *3rd husband of Gwladys
  Laidler* 70, 73
Woodhead, Gwladys *Alhambra proprietor*
  72-73 *see also* Laidler, Gwladys
Worm's Eye View, play 38
The World of J. B. Priestley, revue 50-51
Worth, Harry, *comedian* 79
Worth, Irene, *actress* 79
Wright, David, *architect* 100
Wright, J. T., *building contractor* 8
Wright, Lawrence, *publisher* 65
Wyatt, Alice, *panto star* 14
Wyn, Margery, *actress* 38

Yates, Peter, *film director* 98
Ye Gods, play 16
A Year in an Hour, revue 14
York Minster Appeal Gala 79
Yorkshire Theatres Limited 15

Zack, *dancer* 38